Temptations of the Single Girl

The Ten Dating Traps You Must Avoid

a modern fable

NINA ATWOOD

Temptations of the Single Girl: The Ten Dating Traps You Must Avoid

Published by Wheatmark™
610 East Delano Street, Suite 104
Tucson, Arizona 85705 U.S.A.
www.wheatmark.com

International Standard Book Number: 978-1-58736-898-1
Library of Congress Control Number: 2007930448

This book is dedicated to Mark, my Soul Partner and husband: *Thank you for all of the love and joy you bring into each and every day of my life.*

Books by Nina Atwood:

Be Your Own Dating Service: A Step-by-Step Guide to Finding and Maintaining Healthy Relationships (Owl Books, 1996)

Date Lines: Communication from 'Hello' to 'I Do' and Everything In Between (Owl Books, 1998)

Soul Talk: Powerful, Positive Communication for a Loving Partnership (Sourcebooks, 2003)

As a woman, one of the most important decisions you will ever make in your life is your choice of life partner. Make a poor one, and the consequences could be devastating for years, even decades. Make a good one, and you have the foundation for a lifetime of happiness. Read on if you want to make the right choice.

Contents

Prologue

"Would you like another glass of wine?" Randy asked. Kelly shook her head "no." He cleared his throat. "How is your food?" he asked.

"It's great, really it is," Kelly said, lifting another forkful of pasta to her lips. Inwardly, she fantasized about curling up in bed with the newest Perri O'Shaughnessey novel and a cup of tea. She felt guilty but she couldn't help it. Randy bored her.

He was cute enough, in a clean-cut kind of way, and definitely polite and nice. But he was trying too hard, and there was *no chemistry*. Kelly craved that heart-pounding, bone-melting, skin-tingling kind of passion. With Randy, the conversation was strained, like they were actors struggling to remember their lines. She could scarcely refrain from indulging the compulsive urge to check her watch.

The drive home was endless and awkward. At the first sight of sanctuary, she jumped out of the car, waved good-bye while thanking him for a nice evening, and practically ran into the lobby of her building. Once again, Kelly walked away wishing she'd stayed home and painted her toenails.

* * *

Kelly closed her front door and leaned against it with a sigh of relief. After a moment, she shook herself off and went to the kitchen to make hot tea. She fed Trixie, her calico cat, who loudly purred and rubbed against her ankles. After changing into her favorite pajamas—silk leopard print pants and matching camisole—she curled up on her chaise lounge and opened her laptop, taking a sip of steaming peppermint tea. Her left hand petted Trixie, who rolled onto her back with paws in the air, delighting in the belly rub.

As the computer booted up, Kelly gazed out of her living room window at the sparkling nighttime Dallas skyline. She'd bought this high-rise condo unit primarily for the spectacular city view. Mornings often found Kelly sitting on the balcony watching the sun rise. At the moment, however, she felt overcome by disappointment. How many more dates like tonight's would she endure?

> *"We have more control over the process of finding Mr. Right than we think."*

Once online, Kelly checked her email, scrolling rapidly and deleting the Viagra and mortgage ads. She ignored several messages from clients and colleagues and instead opened an email with an intriguing and rather unusual subject line: "Sharing the Temptations with You—a Gift."

Dear Kelly,

I hope this finds you well. Specifically, I hope you've found "Mr. Right" and are wildly happy. When we met two years ago at Susan's wedding that seemed the only thing missing in your life. I remember our long conversations about the lack of great men over too many glasses of that wonderful Napa wine!

I'm wondering—have you met someone special? If so, catch me up right away with the good news. But if not, please read on. I know this seems odd, but I urge you to take what I have to say seriously.

First, my good news—I'm engaged and getting married in just a few months! I couldn't be happier—Ethan and I are truly soul mates and finding each other is the best thing that's ever happened to me. The truth is, it didn't just "happen" to me; I had to do some serious work on myself so that he could come into my life at the exact moment that I was ready for him. It's not just a coincidence. I discovered that we have more control over the process of finding Mr. Right than we think!

I feel so fortunate to have found real love that I want to share what I've learned with you. I'm referring you to a consultant of sorts who offers a one-on-one program for women like us. She helped me totally shift the way I look at dating, men, and rela-

tionships. The time I spent with this woman was life-changing and invaluable. She taught me about the "temptations of the single girl"—but now I'm getting ahead of myself. You'll find out all about that soon enough.

She charges a rather large fee but don't worry about that because I'm paying yours. I'm offering this to you because someone else who saw my potential did the same for me.

If you decide to accept this offer, you must agree to complete the entire program, start to finish. Secondly, you must agree that if it works for you, you will give it to someone else that you believe it will help. That means that you'll pay the fee at the end, for someone else; trust me, it's paltry when measured against the gain in your life, and you'll be more than happy to refer someone else.

I can't give you the details. You must make the decision based on faith: faith that I'm telling you the truth, and faith that you can accept a huge challenge with a lot of your happiness at stake.

Oh, and one last thing: don't discuss this decision with anyone. You have to make it on your own by looking at your life and examining your heart. I swear there's a reason for doing it this way. It will all make sense later.

That's it! Once you decide, let me know either way. You have 24 hours; otherwise, the program goes to someone else.

Good luck, Kelly, whatever you decide.

Best wishes,

Donna

Kelly slumped back in her seat feeling annoyed. How dare Donna presume so much about Kelly's life and what she needed?

Donna had been one of the other bridesmaids in the wedding of an old college friend. They'd laughed over the atrocious pink dresses they knew they'd never wear again and bonded over wine and long talks about men. Though they had promised to stay in touch, time had slipped away. She hadn't heard from her since Susan's wedding.

Kelly's mind raced. Though happy for Donna, a part of her was envious. Donna had obviously gotten lucky and met the right guy.

How could anyone possibly teach Kelly how to make it happen any sooner than it was meant to be?

Kelly mentally took stock of some of her past relationships. She thought of her college boyfriend, Stan, whom she'd dated for three years. They'd talked about getting married, but when graduation came, Kelly had found herself restless and longing to explore her options before surrendering her freedom forever. Stan had reluctantly agreed to Kelly's wishes. Then she met Ian.

* * *

Ian was the complete opposite of Stan—exciting and passionate and full of adventure. He took her dancing and lured her into dark corners for wild kisses. They impulsively flew to Las Vegas for a weekend, exploring the casinos late into the night, finding clubs and dancing close for hours. They made love over and over. Swept away by Ian's intensity and passion, she broke up with Stan when they returned, convinced that Ian was her soul mate. Stan was angry and hurt. She felt guilty, but she was in love and happy with Ian.

A year later, Kelly longed for Ian to "pop the question," but he never talked about their relationship and she was afraid to bring it up. Suddenly, everything changed. Ian withdrew emotionally and became distant. He partied with his buddies instead of coming over. He insisted nothing was wrong. Finally, she confronted him with an ultimatum: either we work on this relationship or I'm moving on. Ian opted for moving on, claiming that he wasn't ready to commit.

"You're wonderful," he said as Kelly sniffed back tears. "Really, Kelly, it's me. I'm not ready for what you want." Kelly was devastated. She cried for weeks, unable to recover on her own. With the help of a good therapist, slowly she pulled out of the funk of loss.

When Kelly heard that Ian was engaged, six months after their breakup, the grief re-surfaced with the same intensity. How could this happen? Ian had adamantly declared he wasn't ready for a commitment, that it wasn't her. Yet six months later, he was marrying someone else!

* * *

After that, Kelly had held a part of herself back. Over the years, she'd swung between the men she either drove off or broke up with because she didn't really want them and the guys she was wild about but couldn't pin down. There were other chapters in Kelly's love life, too, but some things were just too painful to think about.

After Ian, Kelly had devoted herself to her career. After years of climbing the ranks of a Fortune 500 company, she'd quit and founded her own consulting company. Within a couple of years, she had three employees, freedom with her schedule, choices regarding the clients she worked with, and twice the income of her last job. She traveled when she wanted, gave time and money to her favorite charities, and enjoyed wonderful friendships. Life was good.

Four years ago, Kelly dated Ryan. She hadn't exactly fallen madly in love with him but that was probably healthy, wasn't it? After all, that head-over-heels, weak-in-the-knees stuff had left her numb and broken in the past. Ryan seemed to embody most of the qualities she wanted and they'd had fun together, at least in the beginning. But two years later, after lots of struggling, they'd thrown in the towel.

In many ways dating Ryan had been a re-hash of the relationship with Ian, without the intensity. Their breakup had disappointed Kelly, but hadn't devastated her. She'd convinced herself that she didn't have time for a relationship anyway.

Since then, Kelly occasionally yearned to find someone special but felt powerless. She told herself that going through life solo wasn't bad, in fact it was quite good, and that it was enough.

Kelly rose and walked onto her balcony, her mind churning. She felt unsettled. The part of her that insisted that she didn't need a relationship with a man to feel complete argued with the part of her that wondered if it was true.

She thought of her single girl friends. Though successful and financially secure with plenty of adventure, at the end of the day, usually after that second or third glass of wine, they spoke wistfully of what it might be like to share life with a special man. Later, they rationalized their feelings away with declarations about the impossibility of finding a really great guy and the evidence of past bad relationships as proof.

At Susan's wedding, Kelly had stifled a secret envy of her friend. Susan had glowed and her new husband Mark hadn't been able to take his eyes off her. Kelly had returned from the experience resolved to put more energy into her dating life. She'd joined a couple of on-line dating services and since then had had frequent dates but no real results. There had been a brief fling with a cute guy named Jason but she was so over that.

One sentence in Donna's email resonated in Kelly's mind: "you have more control over the process of finding Mr. Right than you think!" How? She was smart, successful, attractive, and out there on a regular basis meeting new men. Didn't the self-help books tell you that all you have to do is get out there and it will happen? Didn't they tell you that trying to control the outcome was a mistake? She'd learned over and over that wanting it too much was a formula for not having it. She'd read all the books and done all the things advised in them. What more was there?

She had abandoned the idea that she had control over the process when she'd realized that she couldn't make Ian love her the way she loved him. If she were honest, she had to admit that Stan hadn't been able to make her love him either.

All of this left her convinced that love was something you either got lucky enough to stumble into or you didn't. Control had nothing to do with it.

Kelly stalked to her computer and clicked "reply," quickly typing a refusal of Donna's offer. Her finger hovered over the "send" button, and there it stalled. Though she felt tempted to send the email, some-thing held her back. She saved it in her "draft" folder and sighed. She shut down her computer and crawled into bed with Trixie. After lying there for an hour, her mind working, she fell into a restless sleep.

✳ ✳ ✳

The next morning, with a steaming mug of coffee in her hands, Kelly sat on her balcony watching the sun rise. She considered her options carefully. *One, I could hit the "send" button and forget about this*—but that didn't feel right or she'd have already done it. *Two, I could do nothing and let the opportunity pass*—but it wasn't her style to shrink from a challenge.

Three, she thought, *I could take a chance and do this. Why not? My way hasn't gotten me what I want. It's a coaching program, it sounds like, and I've considered hiring a life coach. If Donna could do it, then so can I.*

Besides, if there was one thing she knew about herself, and she knew this down to her toes, it was that she welcomed challenge, even thrived on it.

Ultimately, curiosity prompted Kelly to push the "send" button with an entirely different message than last night's. She thanked Donna for thinking of her, accepted the offer, and asked for her next steps.

Ten minutes later, Kelly's laptop dinged, signaling an incoming email. It was Donna's reply.

> *Dear Kelly,*
> *Congratulations! Martha, the consultant, will be in touch with you shortly.*
> *I wish you all the very best, Kelly! I can't wait to hear back from you when your journey is completed.*
> *Good luck and take care,*
> *Donna*

Kelly closed her laptop and wondered about the ultimate outcome of her decision. Would she be glad she had done this? Would she regret it? Would it be a huge waste of time, not to mention the "rather large fee" she owed at the end? She didn't even know the amount of the fee! Suddenly, Kelly felt shaky, literally trembling inside. What had she done?

Kelly ordered herself to calm down and take it step by step. That was how she'd gotten through big challenges in the past. She thought of that silly old saying: *How do you eat an elephant?* The answer, of course, was: *one bite at a time.* Kelly took a deep breath. After all, what did she really have to lose?

* * *

A week before Kelly's first scheduled meeting with Martha, she received an email:

> *Dear Kelly,*
> *Attached is a list of instructions for you. Please devote some time and thought to the questions asked and bring your answers with you next week.*
> *Below is a preview of our work together. I like to frame this process in terms of the Temptations of the Single Girl, as listed below. You may recognize yourself in some of them but not others, or perhaps in all of them. Our goal is to raise your awareness of the ones that you tend to experience and to teach you how to avoid them. Try to keep an open mind. Don't try to understand all of it just yet. I promise that it will be totally clear when we meet.*
> *I look forward to seeing you next week!*
> *Warmly,*
> *Martha*

The Temptations

First temptation*: Denying your true desires*
Second temptation*: Loving a wounded guy*
Third temptation*: Dating without integrity*
Fourth Temptation: *Choosing high-risk relationships*
Fifth temptation*: Settling for less*
Sixth temptation: *Aiming for the fairy tale*
Seventh Temptation: *Getting sexual too soon*
Eighth temptation: *Rushing into relationships*
Ninth temptation: *Taking the lead*
Tenth temptation*: Sacrificing authenticity*

Kelly read the temptations eagerly, with a surge of excitement and anticipation. She was ready to learn. She was committed to growth. She could hardly wait for her first meeting with Martha.

The First Temptation:

Denying Your True Desires

Chapter One

Kelly sat at one of her favorite restaurants, a chic neighborhood place that specialized in Mediterranean food, as she awaited Martha's arrival. At last, a woman approached her table.

Martha was tall and slender, with light olive skin that was striking with her short, wavy silver hair and blue eyes. She wore wide leg black pants, gold sandals, and a silk turquoise blouse. Her earrings dangled with a bit of sparkle, and she smiled warmly at Kelly as she sat down. Martha could be in her late forties or her early sixties. She glowed with that ageless yet mature, youthful yet sage look that some women were blessed with as they grew older.

"Kelly, it's so good to meet you," Martha said as she took Kelly's hand. When she smiled, her face lit up. It was a face with a model's sculpting, just the right angles and curves, with only a hint of crinkling next to her eyes. Kelly felt a stirring of hope.

"Let me congratulate you on your first step toward growth, the leap of faith you took by choosing to do this program. A huge part of the program is learning to take healthy risks." She smiled again.

"We'll go over the questionnaires I sent you later," Martha said, nodding at the paperwork on Kelly's side of the table. They stopped their conversation briefly and ordered hot tea and a light meal.

After the waiter left, Martha continued. "Today's focus is on our relationship and our contract, but first, I want to get to know you better." She paused again, looked directly into Kelly's eyes, and then asked, "So, Kelly, what *are* you looking for?"

Kelly didn't hesitate. "Love!" she declared.

"And what is love?" Martha asked.

"It's that warm and tingly feeling when you think about him, that I-can't-wait-to-see-you-again kind of feeling. It's wanting to be with him and no one else. It's love! Doesn't everyone know what love is?"

"Everyone has a *feeling* about what love is," Martha said. "But the reality is it's different for each person, and each relationship, like a fingerprint."

"So why are there so many books about what real love is?"

"People want to understand it better because it's so central to our happiness. I've learned that there is a kind of love that is pretty consistent with most happy couples. Right now, though, it's important for you to articulate what it is for you. What is love, in your experience, after being with a guy for a significant period of time—a year or longer? Not what you *think* it is or *should* be, but what it actually felt like for you in the past."

Kelly's smile drooped. "Disappointing," she answered. "It was wanting something I couldn't quite have. It was frustrating, trying to make relationships work, and realizing I couldn't do it."

"How did you get from warm and tingly to disappointment?"

Kelly thought for a moment. "I'm not exactly sure. When I think about my ex, Ryan, for instance, I remember talking about all the things we'd do together, all the fun we'd have. But after dating for a year, he still wasn't ready for a real commitment."

"Okay, let's take it slower," said Martha. "In the beginning, what did you and Ryan agree to in terms of future commitment?"

"In the beginning?" Kelly echoed, confused. "We just wanted to get to know each other. No strings attached, you know?"

"No strings? What does that mean?"

"We wanted to date and just let things happen. We didn't want the pressure of thinking about marriage anytime soon."

"So, you agreed to NOT have a commitment?"

"Of course not! I would never... I mean..." Kelly stammered. Her fingers tightened reflexively around her tea cup.

"We'll come back to that in a minute. For now, tell me what happened after a year of dating, how you felt, what you did. I don't want every single detail, just the essence of it." Martha watched her closely, as if listening to more than the words.

"I was frustrated," Kelly said. "I loved Ryan, and I wanted to plan a life together, but he just shut down." Kelly gazed into her tea as she reflected.

"And?" Martha prompted.

"I thought he needed more time; that I was pushing too hard. But the more time I gave him, the more he backed away. He broke up with me and married someone else a few months later. I just don't understand it." Kelly swallowed over the burning in her throat.

> "*The way you discuss your relationship in the beginning sets the stage, the context, the tone of everything that happens afterward.*"

Martha spoke gently. "Kelly, I want you to take a deep breath, and then I want you to listen very carefully. Okay?"

"Yes." She breathed deeply and felt the tension ease.

"*The way you discuss your relationship in the beginning sets the stage, the context, the tone of everything that happens afterward.* You gave Ryan permission to not work toward a commitment when you said *no strings attached*. Later, when you changed your mind, you changed the rules of the game. You wanted something entirely different and you couldn't understand why he didn't give it to you. But here's the rub: *you set things in motion from the beginning to work out that way.*"

First Temptation: Denial of Your True Desires

Martha paused, allowing Kelly to absorb what she said, then continued. "You didn't really change your mind, did you? If we're totally honest, you hid your true feelings from yourself in the beginning. You wanted a committed relationship leading to marriage, but you didn't acknowledge those feelings or communicate them."

"It wasn't like that," Kelly said defensively. "I really *didn't* want a commitment at first... I, um. I just..."

"Kelly." Martha spoke gently but firmly. "If I allow you to reinforce your old belief, nothing will change, you won't change. You hired me to take you somewhere new, and I will. But you must get *comfortable* with the discomfort of having your beliefs challenged, do you understand that?"

Kelly lifted her gaze from the tabletop and nodded. After a moment, she spoke.

"You're right. I wanted a commitment. I just thought it would work out that way on its own."

"Let's take a hard look at this—it's critical. This is the **First Temptation** that you must learn to avoid: *denying your true desires*. Why would you choose that?"

"I didn't, not consciously," Kelly started to say, battling back the tears she felt stinging her eyes.

"Okay, let's get a couple of things straight." Martha leaned forward slightly, her eyes soft yet intense.

"In order to help you change, I'm going to push you to examine your thoughts and beliefs, and to interrupt them. The goal is to help you *think*, *believe*, and, most importantly, *behave* in an entirely new way so that you can have the life you say you want."

Martha sat back and sipped her tea. "You say you want a loving, committed relationship that leads to a happy, lasting marriage and a family. I'm fully aligned with you on that intention. *I am on your side.* Please keep that in mind. But I need your permission to push you, to make you uncomfortable."

Kelly closed her eyes briefly and absorbed Martha's words. Yes, it hurt, but she believed Martha was truly on her side, that she was there to help her.

"I really do want your help. I can't promise I won't argue with you occasionally, but I am trying. I want you to know that."

"That's fine by me, but I will interrupt you when I see you going down a pathway that reinforces old thinking. Agreed?"

"Agreed!"

The waiter arrived with their food. "Let's eat, and then we'll talk more," Martha suggested. The food was delicious, and they ate quietly for a few minutes.

"Now, there's one more thing we need to agree on," Martha said, "and that is the question of conscious vs. unconscious behavior. My purpose is *not* to help you address your choices and behaviors as unconscious, or stemming out of your painful childhood, and therefore not your responsibility."

As Kelly opened her mouth to respond, Martha held up her hand. "Hear me out first, please."

"I believe our choices and behaviors are conscious on *some* level, even when we feel that they're not. It's hard to accept that because it means taking responsibility for making poor choices in our lives. It means questioning our own motivations and emotional drivers, not to mention values and beliefs. That can be a very uncomfortable journey, but it's absolutely necessary for real change.

"Are you ready for that, Kelly? Take a moment and reflect. Don't say what you think I want to hear. Take your time and answer honestly."

Kelly put down her fork and sat back, eyes downcast, gut clenching. After a minute or so, she looked up, taking a deep breath.

"I feel like my insides are re-arranging. It is uncomfortable. But I'm finally getting the truth, with no room to side-step and make excuses.

"I don't think I can afford NOT to do this. I'm afraid if I keep going down the same old path I'll end up very lonely. I've accomplished all I have so far because I hung in there when other people quit. This is new territory for me and it's scary, but I want to see this through."

> "Our choices and behaviors are conscious on some level, even when we feel that they're not. To accept that means taking responsibility for making poor choices in our lives, and questioning our own motivations and emotional drivers, not to mention values and beliefs."

"Good. Now," Martha went on, "I want you to take a look at why you made choices in a relationship that kept you from getting what you say you really want. Think about it carefully, and ask yourself: *what would I gain from that?*"

"I guess I was afraid that if I talked about commitment too soon it would push him away. Men seem to run from women who talk about that, especially early on."

"That's a good start. But I think there's an even bigger reason you set it up that way." Martha paused. "I'll give you a hint: can a person who's afraid of commitment ask for it from someone else?"

Kelly frowned. "Well, I guess not, but I'm not sure that really applies to me. I mean, it doesn't make sense, does it? If I was afraid of commitment, why would I ask for it from Ryan?"

"My experience is that people *yearn and ask* for commitment because they know deep down that it isn't available, yet desperately need to believe that it is and that it's what they want. All of this, without an understanding of what real commitment is."

"I don't get it. Are you saying that I didn't really want it, so I asked for it knowing I couldn't get it?"

"You tell me. Imagine that Ryan is the one pushing *you* for marriage. Imagine him telling you that he wants a real family and he's tired of waiting for you to decide that you want the same thing. Just picture that, and tell me how you feel."

Kelly imagined the scene and shuddered.

"God, all of a sudden, I remember all the things about him that I didn't like: how he started drinking beer on Saturday afternoons and didn't stop until late that night, the whole time watching sports on television and ignoring me. He wasn't interested in concerts or music or reading books together. We stopped going out on dates pretty quickly; all we did was hang out. It drove me crazy! We weren't on the same page about *anything*."

"And how did you handle the fact that you weren't on the same page?"

"I constantly nagged him to change. He hated that; we fought about it all the time. But what else could I do? He needed to grow up! I wanted to help him. If only he'd listened to me." She sighed. "I guess his wife puts up with his immaturity and bad habits now. That's probably why he married her!"

"What's wrong with that?" Martha asked.

"What's wrong with that?!"

"If Ryan is happy with the woman he married, and she's happy with him, what's wrong with that?" Martha persisted.

"I just don't see how that could be! He's too immature to make a marriage work. I should know; I spent two years trying to change him."

Martha let Kelly stew for a couple of minutes, then spoke gently. "Is that what love is to you, Kelly? Working to change someone?

Pushing him into a commitment that he doesn't want? Where would you be today if you and Ryan were married?"

Kelly thought, and a pained look came over her face. "To tell the truth, I don't like that picture. He'd still be doing all the same things and I'd still be nagging him to change. I'd still feel unfulfilled, only I'd be trapped in a bad marriage with only one way out—a divorce." She sighed again deeply. "I guess I'm really better off without him. We just didn't match."

"Now you're getting it," Martha said gently. "You and Ryan *didn't match*, Kelly, and that means that you couldn't give him what he needed and vice versa. What do you suppose he needed from you that he never got?"

"I guess he needed me to love and accept him for who he is."

"Can you imagine what it feels like to be with someone who doesn't accept you for who you really are? Imagine dating someone who insisted that you lose ten pounds, color your hair, and stop eating meat? Otherwise, he wouldn't really love you?"

"I wouldn't put up with that."

"I wonder why Ryan put up with it for as long as he did," Martha said quietly.

Stunned, Kelly slowly answered. "I never looked at it like that. I guess he really did try in his own way. I remember when we broke up he told me he felt that he couldn't satisfy me. I tried to argue with him about it at the time, but he was right. I wasn't satisfied with him. It wouldn't have worked. Even with the ring and the wedding…" she sighed.

"What did you need from Ryan that he couldn't give you? What do you need to be happy in a marriage?"

"I want a guy who goes in the same general direction as me, without me having to push him. Someone who has the same picture of what our lives should be and who is interested in working it together."

> *"Love is about acceptance. It is seeing someone for who and what he is, and for who and what he is not, warts and all. When you date, you have to look for someone who is easy to accept into your life just the way he is."*

Love is Acceptance

"Okay Kelly, I think you're getting it. Love is about acceptance—it is seeing someone for who and what he is, and for who and what he is not, warts and all. When you date, you have to look for someone who is easy to accept into your life just the way he is. *Acceptance is easy when you match.*

"Dating is about trying on different relationships for brief periods of time until you find someone who feels like a real match. When you fall into the first temptation of denying your true desires, you set yourself up for relationships that don't fit. Then you attach yourself to the wrong people and waste months and even years of your life.

"Most people date whoever shows up next in their lives, choosing them based on attraction, emotional neediness, and little else. Hungry for a relationship, they grab whoever is in front of them and try to force it to work. They either try to change the person, or they ignore the miss-match and forge ahead into marriage. They wrestle over the issue of commitment instead of admitting that they're not a true match.

> *"Real commitment flows naturally when two people fit together, heart, soul, mind, lifestyle, goals, chemistry, and values."*

"Real commitment flows naturally when two people fit together, heart, soul, mind, lifestyle, goals, chemistry, and values. The only reason two people who match might hesitate about commitment is because one or both of them slips out of the heart and into the head where fear rules, but that," Martha concluded, "is a lesson for another day."

"It all seems so obvious now. I never stopped to ask if Ryan was right for *me.* I tried to fit a square peg into a round hole and it hurt both of us."

Kelly went on. "So how do I do this the right way next time? How do I know early on if someone is my match?"

"That, my dear, is the next phase. But first, let's define the terms of our agreement. I have a few rules that I ask my clients to follow, and it's vital that you consider these rules and decide if you can truly agree to them."

After some discussion, Kelly agreed to their rules of engagement:

- Meetings would be monthly on weekends, once on Saturday and again on Sunday; phone calls and emails as needed between face to face meetings.

- They would continue meeting until Kelly's goals were accomplished, however long that took.

- They would create action plans and Kelly would execute them; even if she floundered, she would follow through.

- Kelly would refrain from discussing the program with others—girlfriends, family, anyone—so as to avoid confusion over conflicting advice; Kelly agreed to hash it out with Martha if she disagreed with the advice she gave.

- Kelly agreed not to work with another coach or a therapist during the program; if she felt the need for another person's advice, they would stop the program.

"It's inevitable that another advisor will tell you things that are different from my philosophy," Martha said. "It's not that one is right and the other wrong; you simply need to choose one path and follow it through."

"One more thing," Martha added. "I won't make your choices for you—you have to choose your own path. I will, however, challenge some of your choices. It's vital that you don't withhold from me along the way, even if you choose something you think I won't support. Agreed?"

"Agreed."

"All right. Now I want to give you some pointers that will help you get the most value out of what we do. First, whenever you're faced with an important decision that you feel hesitant about, call me and we'll discuss it. Start using a journal to record the specifics of your dates: what hap-

Tip: "Use a journal to record the specifics of your dates: what happened, significant points in your conversations, your thoughts and feelings afterward, and red flags that you spot."

pened, significant points in your conversations, your thoughts and feelings afterward, red flags that you spot, and so on. Spend time reviewing your notebook before our sessions and zero in on the two or three most important issues for discussion."

Martha went on. "Bring a notebook and your journal with you each time we meet. I'll coach you in new directions that are unfamiliar, so taking notes is vital."

Martha finished by having Kelly sign off on their basic agreements in a simple, one page form.

Next, Martha asked Kelly to review her personal history, specifically her significant relationships, how long they lasted, who ended it, and why it ended. She asked a few questions along the way, but didn't delve deeply into the stories.

Lastly, Martha reviewed the concept of practice. "For me to guide you, you must be in motion, out there, dating and relating. This doesn't work in *theory* but in the actual playing of the game, so to speak. Imagine a football player studying the game on the sidelines but never actually running with the ball. The coach wouldn't have much of a job, would he?" Martha asked.

"Therefore," she continued, "we'll brainstorm ways for you to increase your dating activities. Our goal isn't a race to find Mr. Right and get you to the altar. Rather, we want to put you on the field more frequently, in the game, playing with all your might. The real objective is to increase your *emotional muscle*, meaning your ability to communicate powerfully and make excellent choices. Any questions so far?"

Kelly had none, so they focused on her online dating and other ways to meet men. Martha suggested changes to some of the aspects of her online dating profile (focus on statements about your values, not so much your personal data) and pictures (no short skirts or low neckline shots—it sends a confusing message to men.)

Finally, they wrapped up and scheduled Sunday's meeting. Kelly felt exhausted but hopeful. She really liked Martha's style—she sensed the tough love approach stemmed from genuine caring. She admired Martha's absolute focus on keeping things straight and truthful.

But Kelly couldn't help but wonder if she was truly ready for the challenge. *Will I really be able to do this, or am I just destined to live my life without a relationship?* She sensed her biggest obstacle would be conquering her own self-doubt.

The Second Temptation:

Loving a Wounded Guy

Chapter Two

The following morning, Martha and Kelly met at an upscale health food restaurant with a brunch menu that ranged from homemade granola with fruit and yogurt to a variety of delicious egg dishes. They sat down and ordered coffee and food before beginning their conversation.

Kelly's cheeks flushed and she kept her eyes averted. Martha didn't seem to notice and launched the discussion.

"So, Kelly, what's the most important topic for us to discuss today?"

Kelly consulted her notes before answering. "I'd like to go over my online profile again and make sure that it's the best it can be." She paused. "And then, I, um, want to talk more about how to know that someone is a good match."

Kelly's words sounded a bit hollow, even to herself, but she forged on, rambling about some of the topics she wanted to cover. She even threw in a question or two, which Martha gamely answered.

After they'd finished eating, Martha took a sip of coffee and sighed. "I think it's time to talk about the elephant at our table."

"The what?" Kelly asked, eyes widening.

"The elephant at our table; you know, the one we're tip-toeing around so carefully." Kelly stared into her coffee.

After another minute, Martha gently asked, "Why don't you tell me about last night, Kelly? Who was your late night visitor?"

Astonished, Kelly looked up. "How did you know?"

"It's written all over your face. Who is he?"

Kelly let out her breath, relieved that the subject was on the table, and yet annoyed that she was so transparent.

"His name is Jason. We dated briefly and broke up about three months ago. He came over late last night to talk." Martha asked for details, so Kelly quickly outlined their history.

They'd met through mutual friends at a party and felt instant sparks. He'd asked her to dinner the next night, and they'd lingered over candlelight and wine, talking for hours. Their third date had ended in bed, and Kelly had been totally swept away, convinced that this whirlwind romance was "the one." But the flames had died quickly for him, and four months into it, he'd broken it off. Somehow, Jason had managed to break up with her in such an honest and caring way that she hadn't stayed angry for long. They'd shifted to friends who occasionally had dinner and slept together. The last time they'd done that was several weeks ago. At that point, Kelly had declared that she wasn't interested in sleeping with him unless they were back together, working things out.

Last night, Jason had called and wanted to come over. He'd been out drinking with his buddies. It sounded so lame now, but Jason had turned Kelly's insides soft. He had always had such an endearing way of begging to see her. Last night had been no exception.

✳ ✳ ✳

"Kelly, I miss you. Can I come over? We need to talk about us. Please, Kelly. I miss you."

Fifteen minutes later, she opened the door, immediately enchanted with Jason's boyish good looks, his buff body, that stray lock of hair falling over his forehead, and of course, his infectious grin. As soon as the door closed, he wrapped his arms around her, held her close and nuzzled her neck. Various parts of Kelly's body heated up instantly.

Jason rambled on about his life, his work, and some of his friends' stories, but never once mentioned his and Kelly's relationship. Then, he put on one of her favorite jazz CD's, and pulled her into a slow dance. He swirled her around and dipped her, pulling her close and kissing her. They uncorked a bottle of wine and one thing led to another.

The next morning, Jason held her tenderly and stroked her hair. But all too soon he was up and dressed. Already, she felt him distancing himself. "I'll call you later, Kel, and take you out for dinner tonight," he said on the way out the door. Kelly hoped that maybe, just maybe, things would work out this time.

* * *

Now, sitting here and sharing the story with Martha, Kelly felt foolish. Martha listened attentively, asking a clarifying question now and then. Thankfully, she didn't seem judgmental, and Kelly gradually relaxed.

Martha set down her coffee cup and shifted gears. "Okay, let's discuss your booty call."

Kelly was taken aback. "My what? That's not what it was! Jason and I care a great deal for each other. It just didn't work out the first time around. Maybe it will work out this time."

"Okay, I'll go along with you for a minute on that, Kelly. So, why do you suppose Jason called you last night?"

"He wanted to talk about our relationship. He misses me, and he regrets leaving."

"So, why didn't he do that?" Martha asked. "Why didn't he initiate that conversation?"

"He's scared," Kelly said. "Jason had a really bad marriage in his early twenties. She spent all his money and cheated on him. He got burned really badly and it's going to take time for him to get over that."

"Kelly, if Jason is hesitant to commit because he's been burned, what makes you think he's on the road to recovery? And don't tell me that showing up at your house late at night to have sex with you is evidence that he's changed. You're far too smart for that."

Kelly knew Martha was right. But she couldn't quite give up on Jason, not yet.

"Isn't it possible that he's just afraid? Isn't it true that people can be so scarred from their past relationships that they need time to heal? Maybe all they need is encouragement from someone who loves them."

"That's a good question, Kelly. What you're saying, in essence, is that wounded people deserve our love and compassion, and that when we give it to them, they will make the right choices and do the right things. Is that about it?"

Kelly frowned. "Are you suggesting that I should just write off anyone with any emotional baggage?"

"Of course not. You'll never find a partner with no emotional baggage, but keep in mind that there's *carry-on luggage* and then there are *steamer trunks*. We'll come back to that. But let's delve into this concept of the wounded guy because I think it's important. First, let's switch venues." They paid their bill and left the restaurant, walking through the nearby neighborhood. It was filled with an eclectic mix of beautifully restored cottages dating back to the 1930's as well as a sprinkling of brand-new town houses.

> *"You'll never find a partner with no emotional baggage, but keep in mind that there's carry-on luggage and then there are steamer trunks."*

Loving a Wounded Guy

The walk was good for Kelly. She felt herself relaxing as they strolled along, pointing out architectural features that they liked in the homes they passed, and drinking in the cool late summer morning. Because it was so early, few people were out. It was quiet and peaceful for the heart of a metropolitan area. Eventually, they came upon a quiet little cafe and sat outside with their mocha lattes.

"Okay Kelly, let's get back to our topic. There are basically two types of wounded people. First, there's the *non-intentional* type, who uses his history, whether it's a bad childhood or a bad relationship, depression or an addiction—it doesn't matter what—to avoid responsibility for his life."

She paused before going on. "The non-intentional wounded person believes deep down that he shouldn't have to work so hard because he's had it so bad, or that he can't achieve certain things because it's too hard making the effort. Life is lived *non-intentionally*, meaning that he takes the path of least resistance. He grabs the low-hanging fruit and drifts with no particular goal in mind other than his own gratification and comfort. He typically enrolls well-meaning family members, therapists, friends, and lovers in this dynamic. The non-intentional, wounded person usually has a whole cadre of folks around him trying to get him to change, making life easier for him, and teaching him that he's not accountable for his choices and behavior."

Martha gave Kelly a moment to absorb this. Her tone changed and she looked Kelly directly in the eye.

"Then there's the *intentional* type of wounded person, who views his personal history as just that—history. This person sets goals and intentions for living a life of abundance, success, and contribution to others. He welcomes a challenge, and even though difficulties arise, some of them due to past history, he looks at that as something to overcome. He views his life as a story that *he* writes. Each new day is a new page, each year a new chapter, and *he's the author.*

> "There are basically two types of wounded people. First, the non-intentional type, who uses his history, whether it's a bad childhood, or a bad relationship, depression or an addiction—it doesn't matter what—to avoid responsibility in life. Second, the intentional type, who views his personal history as just that—history. This person sets goals and intentions for living a life of abundance, success, and contribution to others."

"The intentional person lives life with integrity, knowing that the responsibility lies within, not out there. Therapists are utilized to make real change, not just to hold his hand and feel sorry for him. He looks to family members and friends for emotional support, involving them as sounding-boards and reality-checkers. He never uses them to rescue him from his issues and problems. His relationships are a two-way street, and he gives back in full measure."

Here, Martha stopped. She watched Kelly's face carefully, looking for recognition and awareness.

Kelly listened intently. Mentally she viewed the parade of non-intentional men in her past.

"Now, you tell me. Which kind of wounded person are you?"

"I don't think I'm wounded, Martha, but I'm clearly the intentional person. All my life, I've found ways to get past obstacles, and I've done that on my own. It wouldn't even occur to me to expect someone to rescue me."

"We're all wounded to some extent, Kelly. If you don't recognize that, then it's difficult to be honest about the struggles along the way. Someone once said 'No one leaves childhood unscathed.' No parent can give a child *everything* that child needs emotionally, spiritually, and mentally. So even growing up in the best of families, the child within us *feels* misunderstood, thwarted, held back, or neglected, whether that's real or not. All of us carry those feelings into adulthood, whether we acknowledge it or not, blame our parents or ourselves."

"Okay, I get it. Yes, my parents were wonderful, but I'll admit I have some issues that I've worked on in counseling."

"Exactly. Now, which kind of person is Jason? Not what you *want* him to be, or think he *could* be, but rather, based on his *behavior*, in your past experience with him, which is he? I'm asking you to make a judgment call. That's something you've got to be comfortable with as you date men, because your future happiness relies on your ability to do so."

Kelly squirmed. She'd left home that morning with the wistful hope that she and Jason were on the road to getting back together. But Martha's coaching felt like a bucket of cold water. She chose her words carefully.

"I think he's the intentional kind. He finished college and has a good job, so he must have something going for him. He's not into drugs or alcohol, well maybe alcohol a little bit. He does go out drinking with his buddies quite a bit." Kelly trailed off, frowning.

"What about his relationships with women?" Martha asked.

"Jason was a great boyfriend for about three months. He was sweet and attentive. Then he seemed to struggle. One night he came over and sat and cried, telling me he loved me and was trying so hard, but that making a commitment was too scary for him. I felt so much compassion for him. He seemed so hurt from his past."

"What does Jason's past have to do with his not making a commitment to you, Kelly?"

"He's afraid that he'll get hurt again. Making a commitment feels too risky for a guy who's been through that." Even as she spoke, Kelly realized something was missing.

Martha pressed her. "Aren't you at risk when you give your heart, Kelly?"

"Of course I am. We all are, I guess."

"Exactly. And haven't you been hurt in past relationships?"

"Of course I have. I've been truly devastated a couple of times."

"Okay. So, how did *you* overcome your past heartbreaks so that you could make a commitment with someone new?"

"Well, I'm not sure I've overcome it completely. But I want a happy marriage and family, and I'm willing to take some risks along the way to get that. So, I guess it's a decision I've made to risk emotional pain rather than hold back and spend the rest of my life alone."

"Great. Now, why doesn't Jason do the same thing? *What makes him so different?*" Martha stressed the words deliberately and clearly.

Kelly bit her lip. "I don't know. Now that I think about it, I guess I do see him differently, almost like he's got some kind of disability. We've both been burned. But the difference is that I won't let that stop me from having a good relationship now."

"Good. So, why give him a free pass in this relationship? Where does that get you?"

"It gets me back to hoping that maybe this time will be different. Maybe he's changed." As she said the words, Kelly shifted between wishful thinking and dawning awareness and back again.

"What is Jason's motivator for change when he already has what he wants? And I'm not talking about sex. Put yourself in his shoes and imagine how he's feeling today."

"Probably pretty good. I was warm and loving and comforting last night. I made myself completely available and I didn't reject him." Part of Kelly felt good about her loving behavior with Jason last night; another part of her was getting a bit steamed.

"That's right. You gave him all of the emotional goodies of a girlfriend in a committed relationship. What did he offer you in return?"

"Dinner, which may or may not happen. We don't even have

concrete plans!" The dots were connecting, and she didn't like the picture.

"Kelly, the bottom line is that you treated him the way a fiancé, or a wife, would treat him, welcoming him with open arms and giving him unconditional love. In a committed relationship, it would be totally appropriate, but you don't have that.

"Jason has nothing invested in this relationship with you. He has nothing on the line, no commitment offered or made. Doesn't that strike you as out of balance?"

"Are you saying I should withhold love until he commits to me? That sounds manipulative."

"Is it manipulative to not compromise or settle for less than a loving partnership wherein *both people* have their hearts on the line?" Martha asked.

"I guess not. I never thought of it that way. I guess I always thought that if I gave love and acceptance it would come back to me."

"It just doesn't work that way, Kelly. In a real relationship between equals, each step of the way you give to one another, each in your own distinct ways as male and female, gradually building trust and emotional equity in the relationship. It's a process over time and it begins with the first date."

Kelly nodded, fascinated, scribbling notes furiously. It made so much sense. She'd repeatedly felt that she gave herself away with little return on the investment. Now, she was beginning to understand why.

But she couldn't give up on Jason. Surely he was different. She put down her pen.

"I don't know, Martha. All this sounds good in general but... you don't really know Jason. He's a sweet guy and I'm sure he loves me. This feels so judgmental and harsh. Maybe you're off track with this."

"You're right, I don't know Jason, but are you sure that you do? Are you totally clear on where you stand with him and what he wants?"

"I know he loves me and he's trying."

"Is that enough for you, Kelly?" Martha was quiet for a moment, gazing at her steadily.

Kelly stared at her notes and bit her lip. She looked up, letting out her breath.

"I don't know, Martha. This is hard. I'm not sure how I feel."

"Okay, then let's look at this from a different angle. Are you willing to suspend judgment for now and let tonight's conversation provide more clarity?"

"Yes, of course. How can I do that?"

> "In the grips of the second temptation, loving a wounded guy, you hope he'll change, which is frustrating for you both. Even worse, it's not an equal partnership because you're not on level ground."

"First, open your mind to what I'm about to say, even if you don't agree with it just yet. With Jason, you're in the grips of the **Second Temptation:** *Loving a wounded guy.* You hope he'll change, which is frustrating for you both. Even worse, it's not an equal partnership because you're not on level ground."

Martha continued. "The foundation of commitment and devotion is established with someone who matches; an equal partner, not one strong person and one person being rescued. With those basics in place, you focus on the daily loving acts of kindness that bring out the best in each of you. That doesn't mean you never have conflict. It means that your relationship is a top priority for both of you. You don't have to wonder where you stand with one another. All of this takes time to develop but it begins with being absolutely clear about what you want and standing firm about that.

"Do you see how that's different from what happened with Jason last night? Try to picture what life with him will be like in ten years if he continues to behave this way, only now you're married and have children. What do you see?"

Kelly insides flipped over again. She was beginning to realize that her sessions with Martha would be like that.

"I'd be the super responsible person, running a business and raising children while Jason runs around with his friends like a college frat boy!" She sighed. "I don't like thinking of Jason like that." She trailed off, frowning.

"I have something in mind for tonight, something that requires some emotional muscle building on your part. I'd like you to handle this in a way that leaves no room for doubt about where you and Jason stand and the likelihood of a good future. Are you ready for that?"

Dread bloomed in Kelly's throat, but she nodded. "I'm ready," she said.

"Great. Here's what I want you to do." They spent over an hour polishing the plan. Kelly felt prepared to do something radically different from anything she'd ever done before with a man.

✳ ✳ ✳

That night, Kelly and Jason met for dinner. Though he didn't like it, she insisted they meet at the restaurant. They ordered wine and Kelly took small, slow sips, determined to keep her thinking clear. Just in case she forgot something, she had notes tucked into her bag.

Jason romanced her as usual, kissing her hand and scooting his chair close so he could nuzzle her neck. Kelly knew she needed to change this dynamic or she would lose her resolve.

"Jason, we need to talk." As Martha predicted, the comment immediately changed the mood. Jason's smile collapsed and he sat back.

"You're not going to get all serious on me, are you babe?"

"Yes, I am." She took a deep breath.

"I've been thinking, and I've realized that this isn't working for me. I want a committed relationship with someone who loves me the same way I love him. I'm not sure if you're that guy.

"I really do love you but I'm not willing to drift along wanting something you don't. Eventually, I'll resent you for stringing me along and that could blow any chance we might have for a friendship someday."

Jason looked bewildered, but Kelly forged on.

"How do you really feel about me, Jason? Please tell me the truth— I promise you won't hurt me. I'm prepared to hear anything."

"I love you Kel. I really mean that. You're the most wonderful woman I've ever met, but making a commitment is really scary for me. You know what happened in my marriage. I don't ever want to go through anything like that again."

Kelly resolutely tamped down her rising irritation. "What does your marriage have to do with our relationship?"

Jason looked confused. "I'm not ready to think about getting married again. Why can't we just be together now and let the future take care of itself? Isn't it enough that we love each other?"

There it was: the hook that Jason usually cast to reel her in. She took a deep breath and pushed down the anger.

"So you want to date, love each other with no commitment, and let the future take care of itself? Do you ever want to be married again?"

Jason looked annoyed. "I just told you I'm not ready. Can't we drop it for now and just enjoy ourselves tonight?"

"Jason, I need to know where we stand." She stopped, momentarily losing the thread of the conversation. She excused herself and went to the "powder room" where she locked her stall, took deep breaths, and consulted her notes.

Kelly's notes:

- Prepare yourself mentally so you don't react to what he says (no anger or emotional fragility)

- Convey emotional safety so he'll tell you his true feelings

- Be calm and ask direct questions, no side-stepping or soft-soaping

- Don't give him the answers or tell him what to say; ask open-ended questions

- Respond and make decisions based on the reality of what he says and what your gut tells you, not what you wish for

---

When she returned to the table, Kelly assumed a business-like demeanor. Jason looked less and less happy, like a little boy being scolded.

"Jason, please be honest with me, even if you think it will really hurt my feelings. I promise I won't fall apart or anything like that if I don't like what I hear."

"Sure, Kel. Fire away." Jason's voice dripped with dread.

"Thank you." Kelly softened her voice. "Truthfully, when you look ahead, do you see yourself married to me? Do you see us raising a family, growing old together?"

To Kelly's complete astonishment, Jason's eyes clouded with tears. "Honestly, Kelly, I don't know if I see that for myself at all. The thought of getting married again terrifies me. The thought of bringing children into that makes me sick." He looked up at her.

"I wish I could tell you that we'll live happily ever after, but it's all I can handle every day just dealing with myself. I'd make a lousy husband, Kel. You deserve someone who can make your dreams come true. I'm just not the guy for that."

Martha's coaching echoed in Kelly's ears, even as she felt her stomach drop and a dull ache in her heart. "Understanding is the key to letting go of what doesn't work and embracing what does." *Hang in there*, she told herself.

"Maybe someday I'll be ready. Do you think you could wait for me?"

"Exactly what would I be waiting for, Jason?"

"Well, uh, for me to get my act together!" He shifted into teasing mode. "You could teach me, Kel, help me put the past behind me." He gave her his most charming grin.

Kelly simply stared at Jason, whose smile faded. Suddenly she understood that this wasn't a man in front of her, strong and willing to accept responsibility and accountability in life. This was a boy, not yet ready for an adult relationship.

Kelly felt liberated, as if a spell had been broken. She spoke softly, thanking him for his honesty and the time they'd shared. Per Martha's coaching, she kept the drama and tears to a minimum. Jason, though clearly bewildered, accepted Kelly's decision. They parted on friendly terms.

That night, Kelly slept peacefully, knowing that she was on the right path, perhaps for the first time ever.

The Third Temptation:

Dating Without Integrity

Chapter Three

The following Saturday night rolled around and Kelly eagerly anticipated a quiet night at home watching movies. At six, the phone rang unexpectedly.

"Hello?"

"Kelly? It's Kevin. How are you?"

Kelly's jaw dropped. Kevin was at the bottom of her list of likely callers.

"Uh, I'm good, Kevin." She paused. "I haven't heard from you in months."

"I know. Look, Kelly, things have changed. I'm moving out just as soon as I can find a place to live. My marriage is over."

She said nothing.

"Are you there?"

"I'm listening. This is a little hard to believe."

"I know. When we met I was trying my best to tough it out for my kids' sake. I never misled you about that."

"Yeah—I remember. Look, I've got plans."

"Wait! Please don't hang up. I didn't call to rehash all that. I want to talk about the future—our future. Things are finally changing for me so that we can be together." He hesitated. "Unless you've moved on."

Kelly chewed her lip and debated telling him the truth.

"I'm dating," she hedged.

He remained quiet a moment and when he spoke his voice was soft and intense.

"I promise, I'm going to do it right this time. If you don't like what I have to say, I'll leave, but at least give me a chance."

Kelly felt a tug at her heart. Kevin was the one guy she'd loved who embodied every single quality that she admired: he was sweet, sophisticated, confident, a fantastic lover. He was super smart with an Ivy League background and a prosperous career.

He had anticipated her every desire. Incredibly giving and loving, he'd continually surprised her with little gifts and romantic evenings. They'd read books together, gone to the symphony, and philosophized about life, art, and literature. He had even lured her into taking a spontaneous trip to Santa Fe that included a star-filled night at the outdoor opera.

Kelly had truly believed he was her soul mate. If only he could have gotten over his fear of divorcing a woman he didn't love and who didn't love him!

She thought about her last few dates with men she was either (a) bored with, or (b) not attracted to. She reflected on the recent void in her life and how ready she felt to love and be loved by someone special.

Kelly's mind leaped. She imagined life with Kevin as his wife, as the center of his world. Before she knew it, she opened her mouth and invited him over.

Their reunion was sheer heaven. He held her tightly, whispering how much he'd missed her, longed for her. They talked into the night, oblivious of time, gazing into each other's eyes, caressing each other, kissing slowly and passionately.

Kelly struggled to recall Martha's warning about giving herself away too quickly, and somehow managed to tell Kevin that she wasn't ready for sex. "I need to see how this goes," she told him. Reluctantly, he left. They didn't discuss where he went; she knew. But, she told herself, it was only temporary. No doubt he was sleeping on the sofa, and soon he'd have his own place.

The next few days flew by. Kevin came over every night. They went to dinner, lingering over wine and candlelight, talking and laughing. They went dancing, holding each other close. Kelly kept her sexual boundaries in place, sending him away before they got carried away. It wasn't easy. She was falling in love with him all over again.

After their first night back together, Kelly didn't ask questions about where Kevin stood with his separation and divorce. In fact, she'd asked almost nothing that first night except when he was moving out for good. "Soon, Kelly. I've got a realtor looking for a place for me now." She refused to badger him, sure that it was best to let him handle things his way, and in his own time. Meanwhile, she had his undivided attention, and that was enough.

Two weeks passed, then three. Martha's next visit approached, and Kelly seriously considered calling her and canceling the whole program. *Why bother continuing*, she thought. She was with Kevin now, and they were planning their future.

Every night, Kevin built castles in the air for her. "We'll build our dream house together, in Colorado. You can manage your consulting business from anywhere, and I can travel for my work. I'll fly the kids there for visits, and I can see them here when I'm in town for business." On and on he went, saying exactly what Kelly wanted to hear, cementing her conviction that she had found her soul mate.

Three days before Martha's visit, Kelly asked him to spend the night. They made love for hours, and the next two nights were just as wonderful. Kelly didn't ask how Kevin explained not going home to his wife.

Still, something kept her from canceling her session with Martha. The day of her appointment, she told Kevin she had errands to run and kissed him good-bye that morning, promising to re-connect for dinner later. With dread, Kelly drove to meet Martha.

✳ ✳ ✳

After careful consideration on the way to the meeting, Kelly decided to launch a pre-emptive strike. As soon as they ordered breakfast, she took a breath and jumped right in.

"I've found the guy I want to spend my life with, Martha. He's the love of my life."

"That's wonderful, Kelly. So, tell me about him. What's his story?"

"His name is Kevin," Kelly answered. She decided to get the worst over with. "I dated him several months ago and he was married at the time. I didn't know it when we met and once I did, well, it was too late. We fell in love, I asked him to leave his wife, and he backed away. He called three weeks ago and we've been together ever since."

Martha showed no reaction other than curiosity. She asked clarifying questions, quickly uncovering the fact that Kevin was still married and living with his wife and three small children.

Kelly hurried to assure her that he was in the process of moving out.

"Has he filed for divorce, Kelly?" No.

"Has he told his wife about you?" Of course not!

"Tell me again why it's a good idea to date him when he's neither separated nor divorced?" Kelly listed Kevin's many wonderful attributes.

"Okay, Kelly, we could do this a couple of ways. I could try to show you how unlikely it is that Kevin will actually get divorced, become emotionally available, and be ready to marry you in a reasonable time frame. Or I could talk to you about the high probability of second divorce in marriages born out of affairs, not to mention the emotional turmoil that children go through as a result. I could talk about the difficulties ahead of you trying to bond with children who have issues with their father for abandoning and hurting their mother. Not to mention the issue of whether or not he will want more children with you, or even if that's a good idea given the challenges with his kids that are likely to consume your lives for years.

"I could do all of that, but I suspect it won't make a difference to you because it's all an exercise in predicting the future. Neither one of us has a crystal ball. Maybe everything will work out. It isn't entirely beyond the realm of possibility."

Kelly agreed totally. It would be a complete waste of their time for Martha to try to convince her that Kevin wasn't going to fulfill his word to her.

"Instead, Kelly, let's talk about integrity. What does that word mean to you and how does your life reflect it?"

"To me, it means that I'm honest and reliable—that people can count on me to do what I say I'm going to do. That's why I think Kevin is doing the right thing. He doesn't love his wife and probably never has. He should tell her the truth so that they can get on with their lives and be with people they love."

"Let's go with that for a minute, Kelly. If Kevin never loved this woman, how do you explain the fact that he married her and had three children with her? Do you really believe he did all that without any love in his heart? Do you believe he never told her he loved her, affirmed his commitment to her? Or that he said and did those things but didn't mean them? Just led her on for *fifteen years?* What kind of man is capable of that?"

Kelly felt sick at the picture Martha painted. That wasn't Kevin—it couldn't be!

"No, of course not! I don't know what they did together. I suppose he loved her at one time, but it died along the way. He says that she hasn't been a real wife to him in years. They don't even sleep together."

"One thing at a time. Either Kevin loved his wife when he married her and made three babies with her or he didn't. Which is it?"

Feeling cornered, but unable to deny it, Kelly answered, "I guess he loved her. I can't imagine that he would be so cold as to pretend he did when he didn't."

"All right, let's go a step further. Exactly when did this wonderful man stop loving his wife and start having affairs?"

"What?!" Kelly was appalled. "He didn't have affairs—I was the first one, ever."

"Kelly, do you think Kevin tells his wife the whole truth? Do you believe that he goes home to her after being with you and says what a good time he had with his girlfriend? Isn't it true that he goes home and lies to her about where he's been? What he's been doing?"

"I don't like to think of it that way," Kelly said defensively.

Martha watched Kelly intently and continued, "Don't you see that this goes to the heart of his integrity? He lies to his wife and she obviously believes him or she'd have left him by now. What makes you think that you can trust what he says?"

Kelly said nothing, averting her eyes.

"Surely you don't believe that he will always tell you the truth because you are *so special* and lie to her because she's not." Martha let that sink in.

"What gives him the right to view his wife so harshly that he justifies cheating on her and lying to her? If she's *so horrible* as a human being, why did he have three children with her?"

Kelly felt sick inside. She saw the emotional trap into which she'd put herself.

"I want you to put yourself in Kevin's wife's shoes. Imagine that you share three beautiful children with him. Imagine that you're the one lying awake late at night wondering where your husband is, if he's cheating on you, then brushing those doubts aside because you love him too much to believe he would do such a thing. That's how it would be for you, wouldn't it, Kelly, if you were married to Kevin, and he wasn't coming home until 3:00 a.m. night after night?"

"Yes it would," Kelly said at last. "I would never put up with it, though. If any man did that to me, I'd be gone!"

"Without a crystal ball, you can't know what you would do, especially if you had children to consider. Meanwhile, though, I want you to reflect on how you would feel if you discovered your husband was cheating on you."

"Terrible! Hurt, devastated. But Lisa won't find out, Martha. Besides, Kevin isn't leaving her for me; he's leaving her because their marriage is over. He would do the same even if I wasn't in the picture."

"So if you were married to Kevin and he left you, you'd be fine with it as long as he explained that he's not leaving for someone else, he's leaving because he doesn't love you any more? And, by the way, he's *so over you* that he's gone ahead and started a relationship with someone new even though you're not yet separated or divorced?"

"Where exactly do wedding vows fit into this scenario, Kelly? It sounds like you want to get married with the understanding that you'll be faithful only as long as you *love* each other. Is that what you want?"

"No! I mean, yes. I mean…I want to be married to someone who loves me and if he doesn't, I want him to move on."

Integrity—*What's* that *Got to Do with Love??*

"When couples are married for *35 or 40 years*, they often go through long periods of time when they don't feel especially loving toward one another. They may neglect their bond or vent their frustration in other areas of life on each other. Couples are especially prone to this during the early child rearing years. Love, Kelly, is a feeling that waxes and wanes; it isn't a solid thing you hang your hat on. After marriage, real love is mostly about behavior—how you treat one another each day.

"If your marriage goes through a rough patch, what do you want your husband to focus on? Looking for a younger, sexier, prettier woman to comfort him? Do you want him turning to someone who has no history with him and couldn't possibly give him real feedback about his behavior, or do you want him turning to *you* to anchor himself about who he is and what his life is about? Do you want him doing everything in his power to resolve your issues and re-connect with you, or do you want him escaping that responsibility in the arms of another woman? Or into work or alcohol?"

> *"When couples are married for 35 or 40 years, they often go through long periods of time when they don't feel especially loving toward one another. Love is a feeling that waxes and wanes; it isn't a solid thing you hang your hat on. After marriage, real love is mostly about behavior—how you treat one another each day."*

"I want him focused on our marriage, of course," Kelly said. "But what if I've been really awful to him, emotionally beaten him down? I wouldn't blame him if he turned to someone else—I would deserve that, wouldn't I?"

"Do one person's mistakes justify the other person's? What about your future children? How do explain to them your inevitable divorce: 'Sorry about that; I wasn't a good wife so I don't blame him for having an affair and leaving me'?"

Martha paused for a moment, then continued. "Lifelong marriage, Kelly, is about two people doing everything in their power to honor their commitment—that's what integrity is about. They don't react to the other person's mistakes by retaliating, or using each other's mistakes to justify bad behavior or retreating into addictions. *They deal with their issues inside the boundary of their commitment and their absolute fidelity.*

"I want you to look at your own integrity in this situation. How has your behavior contributed to Kevin and Lisa's marital problems?"

Kelly's fork slipped from her fingers and clattered to the table. "What? I'm not the source of their problems, Martha! It's not like I went chasing after him and lured him away from his wife! Their problems existed long before I came along."

"Okay. Let's say Kevin and Lisa had marital problems before he met you. He's upset and confused about how to fix it. Then he meets you and begins an affair. What do you think that does to his incentive to work out his problems with Lisa?"

"I guess it makes it difficult," Kelly said unhappily.

"How could he possibly focus on repairing things with his wife while he's trysting with you? How could he possibly be aware of *his* shortcomings and make amends to her when he's complaining to you about *her* faults?"

Kelly's dismay grew, though her heart clung stubbornly to her love for Kevin. Wasn't it possible that he was really a good guy with a very bad marriage that wasn't his fault? Didn't everyone deserve the opportunity to start over and be happy somewhere else?

But Martha persisted. "This situation goes to the heart of the **Third Temptation:** *Dating without integrity.* Desperate for romance, you go with the flow and abandon integrity, both yours and his. In your case, it's dating a guy who's still married to someone else. It could also be the flip side: dating a guy you know you don't want because he takes you out and treats you well and it's better than nothing.

"Dating without integrity means *doing what feels good today, regardless of who it hurts down the road.* It's grabbing momentary emotional goodies instead of taking an adult, long-term view of the consequences of your actions. It's being self-centered and ignoring the impact of your choices on yourself and others."

She paused before continuing softly.

"Do you really believe that you have the right to interfere in someone else's marriage? Think about how drastically you've altered the dynamics of Kevin and Lisa's marriage. She'll find out about the affair and be devastated, or she'll live with a huge set of lies that obscure the truth about her husband. Either way, the damage is done. Forever lost is the innocent trust they once shared."

> *"Dating without integrity means doing what feels good today, regardless of who it hurts down the road. It's grabbing momentary emotional goodies instead of taking an adult, long-term view of the consequences of your actions."*

Kelly's head throbbed and her throat ached.

"I don't know, Martha. This is too much. I know you mean well. But Kevin's a good guy with a good heart. He's tried to work things out with Lisa but it isn't possible. He did try.

"He loves me, Martha. I know some married men cheat and lie— they're not good guys. They do it because they don't care about their wives or anyone else—they just use women. But that's not Kevin! He wants a life with me and he'll do the right thing by Lisa. He's got a plan for how to manage the divorce so she and the kids are financially taken care of. You just don't know him, Martha."

Kelly's face flushed and her breathing was rapid.

"Okay. I can see that you're overwhelmed. Let's break for the day and meet again tomorrow. What do you plan to do tonight when you see Kevin?"

"I don't have any plans except to enjoy being with him," Kelly stubbornly replied, refusing to look at Martha.

Martha was quiet for a moment. "Well, that is one tact you could take. Are you open to hearing another idea?"

"I don't know, Martha. Kevin and I love each other and you promised you would support me. Accusing Kevin of being a cruel, unloving liar is hardly supportive."

"I do support you, Kelly," Martha said softly. "I support you in your goal of having a great relationship. I know this conversation isn't easy but the goal is the same. I promise you that if you come through this with Kevin and you're happy, I'll be right there cheering you on."

Kelly's eyes stung with unshed tears. "I love Kevin. I don't want to lose him."

"Loss is painful; I know that better than anyone." Something in Martha's tone of voice caused Kelly to look up. She caught a faraway glint in Martha's eyes just before her tone turned serious again.

"The point here is to face the reality of the situation, Kelly. If that reality is a good one, we'll go with it. If not, we have to deal with it. OK?"

"Of course," Kelly said, thinking to herself, *I know what the reality is. And I've already chosen.*

"Good. So what is your plan?"

"I guess I'll ask him a few more questions about where we stand and what his plans are." Kelly sighed, clearly not happy about where this tactic might lead.

On her way home, Kelly tried vainly to collect her thoughts and make sense of the session. A part of her understood that Martha wanted her to see that Kevin's marriage mattered, not just to Lisa, but to his children and to him as well. She realized that she'd been in denial about a huge part of Kevin's life. Still, she couldn't quite bring herself to acknowledge how it might impact his ability to love and commit to her.

She wanted to retreat to the cozy cocoon of love she'd inhabited for the past three weeks. She wanted desperately to believe that she and Kevin would make it work. The thought of losing him again made her sick. She couldn't imagine ever loving anyone as much as she loved Kevin; ever again feeling such compatibility on so many levels.

✳ ✳ ✳

That night, after two glasses of wine and with much effort, Kelly forced herself to bring up the subject.

"So, when are you moving out?" Kelly asked, trying to sound light but failing miserably.

"Soon," he said, handing her a cracker with cheese on it. "Umm, this is great," he said, munching away on his. "How about another glass of wine, Sweetie?"

"Kevin, I really want to know what's going on."

"Don't worry, Kelly, everything's moving forward. It will all work out, okay baby? We're together and I'm not going anywhere. I love you and that's what matters, isn't it?"

"I know you love me, but I still need more information. When are you filing for divorce? Have you found a new place? When do you move in? And how is Lisa taking all this?" Kelly was on a roll.

Instantly, his mood darkened.

"I told you I'm doing the best I can. You either trust me or you don't. Is this going to be the way it is with us—you always questioning me? Second-guessing me? I've had enough of that to last me a lifetime."

The subtle threat lurking beneath Kevin's words paralyzed her. Quickly, she smoothed it over.

"No, no, of course not, Kevin! I know you're doing the best you can. I'm just so ready to start our life together. I love you and I want to share everything with you."

Kevin, mollified, wrapped his arms around her. "I know, baby. Me, too. Don't worry, everything will be okay." For a minute, he held her tenderly and hope flickered again. The knot in her stomach let up just a little. His lips found hers and he kissed her passionately.

Kelly felt torn. Part of her yearned for something she suspected Kevin couldn't give her. The other part of her wanted to escape into the carefree abyss of their passion. She pushed her fears aside and gave in to the warmth and excitement of Kevin's touch.

Later, Kelly lay awake in the dark thinking about Kevin's wife. Against her wishes, Lisa was becoming real to Kelly. She was no longer just an object in Kevin's life, a cardboard cutout of a woman, soon to be tossed aside.

Kelly wondered about her. *Is she like me? Could she be a woman wanting more from a man than he can give her, a woman with an aching heart?* She empathized with her. No one knew better than Kelly what a broken heart over a man felt like.

Kelly studied Kevin's profile as he lay fast asleep beside her. How could he be so peaceful when the two women in his life were in so much pain? After a long while, she fell into a restless, uneasy sleep.

The Fourth Temptation:

Choosing High-risk Relationships

Chapter Four

Sunday morning, Kelly awoke to an empty bed. Panic stabbed at her heart. Quickly, she dragged on sweats and stumbled into the living room. Relief washed over her when she spotted Kevin out on the balcony, sitting in one of her chaise lounges, his back to her. She let out a shaky breath. *What an idiot I am*, she thought. *Get a grip Kelly!*

As she approached the patio doors, Kelly realized Kevin was on his cell phone, talking earnestly. She hesitated by the doors, which were open just a crack.

What she heard made her heart pound anxiously. "Okay, okay, Lisa, calm down." He said more, but she couldn't catch it.

"It's all right…" and "yes" and "okay, I'm coming home right now." He listened for a long time, said a few more words very softly, and then disconnected. He sat still for a couple of minutes, gazing into the distance. Then he stood up, turned around, and saw her.

"Kelly! I didn't know you were up." He came back into the living room, pulling the patio doors shut behind him. "How did you sleep?" he asked, as if it were just any ordinary Sunday morning.

Kelly felt stricken, almost paralyzed with fear. All she could manage to say was "I heard you. You were talking to Lisa, weren't you?" Kevin tried to reach out and take her hand, but she snatched it away.

"Don't do that; don't pretend it was nothing. I saw your face, I heard your voice. *I know something's up*—tell me!" Her voice rose with each sentence until she was nearly shrieking.

"Kelly, sit down, let's talk. Don't look at me that way. Come on." He pulled her down next to him on the sofa.

"That was Lisa." His voice had a mechanical quality and he couldn't seem to look Kelly in the eyes.

"One of her friends saw us come here last night." He paused, and Kelly's heart plunged.

"The thing is, Kelly, she's really upset. She's hysterical, crying, screaming. My kids are with her. I can't let them see her like that. I have to go home and calm her down."

"I don't understand—why is she so upset? Surely she realizes that since you're getting a divorce you might be dating." Kelly tried desperately to rationalize what was happening.

"I can't do this right now. I have to think about my kids—they come first. They're just kids, Kelly! They aren't old enough to understand what's happening. I need to be there, take care of them, protect them. I know you don't have children but if you did, you'd understand."

Kevin's words cut her to the quick. What was he saying? Was he accusing her of not caring about his children? How could he think that of her?

"I may not have children but I can understand they're upset. Don't you think it has something to do with how Lisa behaves? Doesn't she have the maturity to control herself in front of her children? This isn't your fault!"

Kevin looked at her as if he didn't know her. "It doesn't matter whose fault it is. What matters is my kids. I'm going home to make sure they're okay."

Tears stung her eyes and though she struggled to hold them back, it was impossible. He was leaving! After all his declarations of devotion, he was leaving to be with his wife. Again.

"Kelly," Kevin said softly. "Kelly, don't cry. It's all going to work out. This is just a speed bump. Don't worry." He hugged her and she cried on his shoulder. Then, he gently disengaged and stood to go. Within minutes, he was out the door, peppering her with reassurances as he went. None of his words stopped the pain in Kelly's heart.

* * *

Kelly didn't know where to begin with Martha. She was grief-stricken yet her feelings didn't make sense. Kevin had assured her he wasn't leaving. He'd be back tomorrow or the next day, once the storm subsided, and his kids were okay. She trusted him to keep his word. Didn't she?

But sitting here with Martha, she was embarrassed. How could she continue to defend her decision to be with Kevin? What would Martha think now?

"Kelly, what's going on? You're obviously upset." Martha probed in her usual gentle, direct way.

"I'm not sure what to say, Martha. Everything was great with Kevin last night. We were closer than ever."

"Did you discuss his timetable for moving out?"

"Well, he didn't have one. He got pretty defensive." She hesitated.

"When I questioned him, it felt like he was angry, like I had done something wrong. Maybe that has something to do with this morning."

"What happened this morning?"

Kelly told her about Kevin's phone call and abrupt departure. "He said it's just a 'speed bump,' so I don't know why I'm so upset." Her eyes began leaking tears again.

"Why *do* you feel so sad, Kelly?" Martha asked.

"I guess I can't help feeling that he's leaving me. Even though he said he wasn't, I'm afraid he's going to be lured back into the relationship with Lisa, out of fear and guilt." Kelly looked up at Martha, suddenly stricken. "Maybe I drove him away, Martha! I pushed too hard, made him think I didn't trust him!" That brought a fresh wave of tears. Martha waited for Kelly to calm down.

"I know you believe right now that Kevin is your soul mate and that you may be losing him, but the reality is that Kevin's been married for many years to Lisa. Regardless of how he feels about her now, at one time he loved her and made babies with her. That's a lot of emotional glue, Kelly. Like it or not, Kevin's first loyalty is to the family he has now."

Kelly flinched at Martha's words, at the unavoidable truth in them. Martha paused while Kelly absorbed it all.

"Kevin has a *responsibility* to his family that far outweighs any promises he made to you. Maybe if you'd met him early in his marriage, before there were babies, and he and Lisa lacked common values, or she annihilated their vows with drug or alcohol abuse or infidelity, then things might be different. He could admit he'd made a mistake and get out with relatively little damage.

"But that's not the case here, Kelly. He's a married man with children—a family he consciously created. It's too late for him to use the excuse that he's not compatible with Lisa, that he made a mistake marrying her. He *chose* this path, and now his duty is to honor her, their commitment, and their children.

"If he left her and his children in order to marry you, your marriage would be founded on infidelity and betrayal. That's a shaky foundation on which to build a life. How can you feel secure with him knowing he abandoned his first family? How could you sleep at night knowing his children suffer because their Daddy left them to pursue his own selfish needs?"

Kelly wanted desperately to defend Kevin. She wanted to believe that it could work—that he could leave his wife and children and everyone would be okay. But she couldn't escape the truth of Martha's words. Hope ebbed away.

"Kelly, why would you choose this?" Martha studied her intently. "What is it you're seeking to resolve through this relationship?"

Kelly sat still, letting the question sink in. Slowly, she began to talk.

✳ ✳ ✳

After a girls' night out, Kelly met Kevin while waiting for the valet to bring her car around. He was amazingly good looking and he seemed utterly enchanted with her. He asked her to stay and have one more drink. She did, and the sparks were instant and overpowering. He went home with her that night. It was the beginning of an electric affair, charged with intensity. They saw each other every day after that, though oddly, he always left in the middle of the night with excuses about early meetings he needed to prepare for.

Later, when he admitted he was married, it was too late for Kelly to back pedal. She was furious, but he held her close and said all the right things—that he wished he'd met her before his wife, that his marriage wasn't good and he wanted out. Hope surged in Kelly's heart and she decided to give Kevin time to resolve his feelings and get a divorce.

At first, Kelly felt more powerful than she'd ever felt as a woman. Kevin pursued her with unrelenting attention, calling every day, begging to see her, sending flowers. She teased him about her calendar filling up with other dates. When she saw him, he couldn't keep his hands off her.

Before she knew it, Kelly was in love. She would never forget the night he told her he loved her. "I'm not happily married, Kelly. I want out, but I can't leave my kids yet, not while they're so little. They still need me. I can't imagine not being there every night to tuck them in." He cried, and Kelly held his hand, assuring him she would wait.

The balance of their relationship shifted after that. Kevin was still attentive, but Kelly lost the sense of goddess-like power and began feeling like a needy child, always craving more.

Then Kevin dropped the bomb on her. "I can't do this. I feel torn between my life with my kids and you, Kelly. It's killing me. I miss you when I'm not here, and I ache for them when I am." He ended their affair, and Kelly's heart shattered into a thousand pieces.

✳ ✳ ✳

Kelly swallowed a sob and blew her nose. "I can't believe I'm going through this again!" she wailed, struggling to regain control.

"You asked me what I'm seeking in this relationship. I want to believe I made a good choice by loving Kevin. I want to feel special and valued! I want to be the one he chooses."

"So you want validation both for your choice and for your own worth. That's a powerful realization, Kelly. Knowing that you want to feel special and valued is important because *that's your emotional driver*. But tell me, why do you choose men who can't or won't give you what you want?"

"I don't know!" Kelly blubbered. "I just don't get it! They seem to love me, and then poof! They're gone!" She felt terribly confused, as if a huge insight hovered just beyond her reach.

"I'm not sure I can do this. It's too hard. I just keep making one stupid mistake after another." Her shoulders sagged with defeat.

"I think we need a break. Let's find another place to talk. I have an idea for something that might help you feel a little better."

Choosing High Risk Relationships

They drove a few blocks to the Nasher Sculpture Garden in the arts district of downtown Dallas. They strolled through the lush green grass of the outdoor garden, gazing at each magnificent sculpture.

Martha spoke soothingly, relating the story of Raymond and Patsy Nasher, their shared passion for art, their partnership in collecting, and his undying devotion to his wife. Even after her untimely death, he had continued collecting as a tribute to their life together, ultimately creating the sculpture garden.

Kelly listened, took deep breaths of fresh air, gazed at the crystal blue sky, and wiggled her toes in the grass. Slowly, her heart lifted as she imagined this devoted couple traveling the world together, raising a family, and leaving behind this phenomenal legacy.

"Why do you suppose I'm sharing this story with you, Kelly?" Martha asked.

"I guess you want me to hear about a happy couple and their life together. It makes my heart ache when I compare it to my situation with Kevin. I wish we could have what they had." Kelly felt such deep longing.

"Yes, Kelly, but there's more. I want you to reflect on what it is about some women that they attract loving, devoted men. I don't want you to think that it's about her looks, or even how smart she is. I want you to reflect on the *inner qualities* that make a woman appealing to a man who is capable of that kind of devotion."

Kelly thought about it for a few minutes as they walked.

"She likes herself, values herself. I've always believed that a woman with good self-esteem is attractive. But I've always felt great about myself, so I don't get how that applies to me."

"How good do you feel about yourself right now?"

Kelly answered in a small voice, "not very."

"Did you feel any alarm bells going off somewhere in the back of your head when you hooked up with Kevin again?"

Looking down, Kelly answered sheepishly, "Yes, but I went ahead anyway."

"What you've done with Kevin is given in to the **Fourth Temptation:** *choosing high-risk relationships* that feel good today but devastate you tomorrow. When you do, you sacrifice your own self-care.

"The worst part of your pain is that it's self-inflicted. Those warning bells are there for a reason. It's the wiser part of you trying to rein in the willful child. When you ignore the warnings, plunging recklessly ahead, you ditch your self-care.

"A woman with good self-esteem, Kelly, simply does not put herself in this position. She looks at the big picture, reads between the lines, and isn't swayed by momentary passion. You can fall in love with almost any man you are attracted to! But choosing *an emotionally available man with good character* to love and be loved by is an entirely different matter.

"It takes really good self-esteem to pass up a charming, attractive guy who seems to offer some instant romantic goodies, but with a huge price tag attached. I'm talking about every kind of emotional unavailability."

Kelly knew she had sacrificed the big picture in order to feel loved, however briefly. Looking back, she saw how quickly she'd grabbed what Kevin offered, never really considering the consequences.

Martha continued. "The next few days are going to be tough, Kelly. Expect to go in and out of reality and denial. One moment you'll see this for what it is: an

> *It takes really good self-esteem to pass up a charming, attractive guy who seems to offer some instant romantic goodies, but with a huge price tag attached. You can fall in love with almost any man you are attracted to! But choosing an emotionally available man with good character to love and be loved by is an entirely different matter.*

> *Tip:* "*Pursue a life in which no man, no matter how attractive or charming, can ever again displace your commitment to self-care.*"

untenable situation you must purge from your life so you can move forward. The next moment, you'll find yourself grieving, longing for Kevin and rationalizing that it could still work.

"I want you to reflect on the really big job you have of anchoring your self-esteem once and for all. I want you to imagine a life in which no man, *no matter how attractive or charming*, can ever again displace your commitment to self care."

Martha paused before adding the final note. "This isn't about ordinary disappointment and loss after breaking up. That happens sometimes, and it stings.

"This is about the devastation that results from choosing a person or a situation that's bad for you and getting hurt as a result of your own choice. The real damage is the self-punishment, the self-doubt, and the drop in self-esteem, all because *you did it to yourself*, ignored your own alarm bells.

"For now, just take that in and reflect. Let the wiser, more self-aware part of you have a voice.

"Don't beat yourself up over this, Kelly. That only compounds the problem. Instead, be responsible and accountable, looking at your choices and behavior in a dispassionate way, taking note and owning up. Will you do that?"

Kelly agreed that she would try. Martha gave her some specific instructions for what she called "radical self-care" and extracted her commitment to fulfill them. "Hang in there!" Martha whispered in her ear as she hugged her goodbye.

Kelly drove home feeling utterly exhausted. She drew a hot bubble bath and lit candles, per Martha's instructions. As she soaked with her head back, a cold washcloth over her eyes, Kelly recalled Martha's parting words. "Care for your self the way you might a beloved

> "*The real damage of choosing high-risk relationships is the self-punishment, the self-doubt, and the drop in self-esteem that results because you did it to yourself by ignoring your own alarm bells.*"

daughter, for that is who you are: a cherished daughter of the universe."

Kelly felt fresh tears, but this time, it wasn't just grief over Kevin. Her heart could barely hold the reflection of her true value in Martha's eyes. What did it mean? Why did that touch her deep inside in such a bittersweet way? Sighing, Kelly let her thoughts drift. She slowly released some of the pain and tension. Later, she climbed into bed and fell into a deep, dreamless sleep.

* * *

The next few days dragged on endlessly. Each morning she woke to the crushing reminder of Kevin's departure. That usually brought a fresh wave of grief followed by a feeling of heaviness that remained in her heart throughout the day.

Every day, Kelly hoped to hear from him. As each day ended without a call, she fell asleep sad and despairing, only to hope again the next day.

Sometimes, Kelly remembered Martha's words, about integrity, commitment, and loyalty to his family, but she found it difficult to focus on those thoughts. She didn't want to believe that loving Kevin was not in her best interest.

What is the reality here? Is it wrong to want things to work out with the man I love? She felt so conflicted. Occasionally she glimpsed moments of clarity, but then the smokescreen of longing and grief obscured whatever she briefly saw.

* * *

Kelly was sitting on her balcony with her wireless laptop, sorting through email, when the phone rang. Her heart leapt.

"Hello?" Somehow, she knew it was Kevin, even before he spoke. His voice sounded so different, so distant.

"Kelly, it's Kevin. I'm calling to tell you I can't see you anymore." He sounded completely detached, and Kelly's heart plunged. She began to tremble and clutched the phone more tightly in her clammy fingers.

"Kevin? Why are you talking to me this way? Please, come over so we can talk in person." Kelly felt desperate.

"I'm not coming over today or ever again. My wife and I are working things out. I don't want you to call me anymore. Don't show up at my office or call or email or anything like that ever again. Do you understand?"

"What are you talking about, Kevin? You know I don't…"

He cut her off. "It doesn't matter what you say, Kelly. I don't want you in my life." He disconnected.

Kelly slowly hung up the phone, in complete shock and disbelief. Her mind was in disarray. She couldn't think coherently. Her heart pounded and she had difficulty catching her breath. She felt like she might die.

Somehow, she managed to sit down, put her head between her knees, and take gulps of air until the feeling passed.

Kelly groped for her phone and dialed Martha's number, praying that she would answer. She did, and Kelly poured out the whole story. Martha listened compassionately.

"Keep taking deep breaths, and let's try to make sense of this. Did it sound like maybe Kevin wasn't the only one on the phone?"

Comprehension slowly dawned.

"Yes, it did. His voice sounded the way it does when someone knows that he's being listened to. What he said didn't make sense. He made it sound like I'm some kind of fatal attraction head case! I never called him at work or anywhere else. He always initiated contact. I wouldn't dream of showing up at his office uninvited and he knows it!"

"Kelly, is it possible that his wife was on the line?"

"I don't want to believe it, but it looks that way." *How could he do that? How could he put her in the position of looking like a scheming, stalking, husband-stealing whore?*

"Why would Kevin do this, Kelly? Think about it."

She didn't want to, but Kelly couldn't help seeing the cold, hard truth.

"He's obviously trying to put his marriage back together. She probably asked him to call and break it off with me while she listened to make sure that he really did it."

"What does this tell you, Kelly?" Martha gently asked.

"You were right all along: his first loyalty is to the family he has now. And he's a coward! He threw me under the bus to save his own hide! He didn't even have the guts to tell his wife the truth about us, to give me the dignity of at least saying good-bye in a way that respects me and what we shared."

Kelly felt so defeated. Just a few short days ago Kevin had held her in his arms and told her she was the love of his life. Now, she was simply the discarded "other woman," scorned and degraded by his final act.

"Is there any part of you that believes Kevin's behavior reflects real love?"

"No," Kelly answered quietly. She could no longer escape the truth. Kevin didn't really love her, not in the way that mattered.

Kelly cancelled her work for the remainder of the day, handing over the essential projects to her staff. The grief and sadness were overpowering. She'd never felt so alone in her life.

The next few days were a mind-numbing blur of shock, grief, and sadness. At times she felt hopelessness and despair, but she focused on putting one foot in front of the other. She tried to remember Martha's words, though it was hard to believe them. "Even though it doesn't seem like it, this pain will pass. And when it does, you'll have the opportunity to carve out a whole new perspective on your life, your goals, and how your relationships with men fit into them. As painful as this experience is, the clarity and insight you'll gain from it will be vital to unraveling your old patterns and establishing new ones.

"One of the biggest issues for you Kelly, is getting too attached to the wrong men. To achieve your goal, you have to shift to an attitude of detachment balanced with an open heart, though that may seem paradoxical right now."

Martha then gave Kelly some

Tip: "Create a mantra and commit to speaking and meditating on it every day. Over time the mantra will help you release the emotional baggage and gradually recognize the truth of any situation."

homework that at the time seemed unimportant but later would turn out to be a powerful tool that would change everything in Kelly's choice of men. She called it "The Mantra," and instructed Kelly to write, speak it, and meditate on it every day. "If you use it now, and every time you're dating someone you have feelings for, your choices of men will radically change for the better."

Kelly's Mantra:

(Write and meditate while focusing on the current man in your life)

[Name] will either love me or he won't

He will be faithful or he won't

He will commit to me and to our relationship or he won't

He will be committed for a short time or for a long time

Over his choices and behavior I have no control

I recognize that my only control is over my own thoughts, feelings, behavior, and choices

I release the illusion of control over the outcome of this relationship

If it is in my highest and greatest good* to be with this man, then I ask for us to move into a commitment quickly, easily, and naturally with no effort on my part

If it is not in my highest and greatest good to be with this man, then I ask for release from my attachment to this relationship

*Highest and greatest good = healthy; values that match; equal love and desire for the relationship so that it's emotionally balanced; life goals and purposes that match so that it's highly likely you will be happy for a lifetime; feels good to be together not just in the physical, erotic sense, but in the sense of adding joy and positive contribution to one another's lives on a day-to-day basis

---

The Fifth Temptation:

Settling for Less

Chapter Five

Kelly followed Martha's instructions to the letter, though it wasn't easy. Each day, she walked briskly for 45 minutes. After that, she sat in her living room with no distractions and practiced deep breathing with her eyes closed. The goal was to achieve a meditative state, something that she wasn't familiar with.

Martha asserted that Kelly lacked clarity about who she was and what her life was supposed to be about. Meditation, she said, was one sure pathway to getting in touch with that.

"What you're missing, Kelly," Martha shared in one of their brief check-in calls, "is an inner compass when it comes to men: a reference point for how you live that you don't violate, no matter what. In the past, you've chosen men who extended the *hope* of being loved, but always with a fatal flaw that you overlooked out of desperation.

"Your inner compass should contain all of the information you need to make a good judgment call when you're dating someone new. That way, you don't give away your heart, soul, and body to the wrong kind of men, setting yourself up for emotional devastation. Meditation and your mantra help you set that compass on due north."

Kelly meditated daily, ending the sessions with notes in her journal. She repeated her mantra, though it didn't make sense right away. She focused on Kevin when she did it, even though they weren't together. "The mantra helps you release the emotional baggage and gradually recognize the truth of a

"Your inner compass should contain all of the information you need to make a good judgment call when you're dating someone new so you don't give away your heart, soul, and body to the wrong kind of men and thereby set yourself up for emotional devastation."

situation," Martha told her. "Use it when you're with someone, and use it when you're still emotionally attached, especially when there's pain involved."

At first while meditating, all she could feel was pain and confusion. Her mind raced. Gradually, her thoughts slowed as she learned to focus on deeper and slower breath.

In her journal, she wrote pages and pages of emotional dumping about the men in her past. She rambled on and on about their self-centeredness, their faithlessness, and their dishonesty.

One morning Kelly stopped writing as a strange thought popped into her head. She quickly scanned the previous ten pages of her journal and counted the number of times she'd written the word "he" (or a derivative of he) or a man's name: one hundred and thirty seven.

One thing is for sure, she thought, *I'm practically an expert on him! Apparently, I know all his thoughts, feelings, all of his wounds from childhood forward!*

Where is the part about me? Where are my feelings, my thoughts, my motivations? She resolved to stop writing about all the "he's" and instead, write about the "she" sitting right there. As she focused more on her mantra and on the concept of what was in her highest and greatest good, the obsessive thoughts about men, past and present, gradually loosened their grip on her mind.

But she wasn't out of the woods yet emotionally. As the days went by, Kelly's feelings shifted from sadness to anger and back again. Her mind was restless; it was as if a whole committee had taken residence there, holding endless meetings with no resolution. She felt exhausted at the end of each day but slept restlessly at night.

Kelly hid in a social cave. She stopped returning calls and let emails go unanswered. She had absolutely no desire to meet anyone new and she certainly didn't want to go over this sad chapter of her life with well-meaning friends who would either pity or judge her.

She felt embarrassed as she realized how blatantly she had ignored red flags time and again, plunging recklessly ahead, motivated by a desperate need for love and a complete unwillingness to say "no" when even the most remote opportunity for love presented itself.

Kelly saw that most of her relationships were characterized by a sense of urgency. She'd slept with men almost as soon as she met them. She'd taken no time to get to know them, their true character, or their joint values before giving away her heart. She'd mistaken passionate kisses and grandiose gestures for real love. She'd asked very little of men, but had given back a ton of unconditional love.

She saw the pattern but wasn't sure she could change it. She wondered if the cynicism of some of her single women friends was justified. Perhaps there simply were no good, single guys out there. Maybe a great relationship either didn't exist or was too much to hope for. The grief was overwhelming in its intensity and shook her to the core.

One night on the phone with Martha, Kelly voiced her sense of hopelessness. "I don't know, Martha. I'm not sure I can do it. I think my 'chooser' is broken. Maybe I'm better off without a relationship. At least that way my heart won't get broken again and I won't hurt anyone else."

"Kelly, your feelings are normal following a devastating break up. Trust me—it's only temporary. Besides, there really isn't an option for not having a relationship with a man."

"What do you mean? If I decide not to fall in love again, why can't I do that?"

"Because falling in love isn't something you can control. You either do or you don't with the person in front of you. You can't *make* yourself love a guy that you don't love, and it's not easy to *stop* yourself from loving a guy that you do. Whether or not that love is *real* is another story. The point is that you may have the feelings even if you don't want them.

"You fall in love by spending one on one time with someone that you're attracted to. So if you don't want to fall in love, you have to give up dating because dating leads to those kinds of feelings.

"If you don't want to date, you have to give up socializing because that leads to meeting single guys who are bound to ask you out. Can you imagine yourself in front of a totally hot guy who's begging for a date and telling him 'no' because you've decided you don't ever want to date again?"

Humor laced Martha's voice and Kelly had to admit the truth of what she was saying. Okay, so she wasn't going to give up socializing and yes, that was bound to lead to dating again. How, then, could she protect herself from pain in the future?

Settling for Less

"The goal isn't to prevent pain, which is a part of life because we are constantly confronted with loss. You lose your watch and feel disappointed; you lose a family member and grieve for a long, long time."

Martha's voice faltered a bit as she said this. Kelly wondered what it meant, but before she could think about it, Martha cleared her throat and went on.

> *Tip:* "Set yourself up for success by making certain discernments about men: their character and emotional availability. Cultivate your own inner strength and clarity of vision so that when dating you will have the ability to challenge a guy when necessary and let go when it's clear you're on the wrong path."

"Pain is a part of life. *Suffering*, however, is optional, and I don't mean the kind from unpredicted trauma over which you have no control. I'm referring to the suffering we create through our own foolish choices and distorted ways of thinking.

"The goal is to learn how to set yourself up for success by making certain discernments about men: their character and emotional availability. Secondly, it's to date men from a position of inner strength and clarity of vision. That gives you the ability to challenge a guy when necessary and let go when it's clear you're on the wrong path.

"What we're aiming for is ordinary loss and disappointment at most, because sometimes things just don't work out, not the devastation you feel right now. That way, you quickly pick yourself up and get back in the game.

Temptation: Settling for Less

"If you don't get out of your old path, you fall into the **Fifth Temptation:** *Settling for less* than a really great relationship. You settle when you desperately attach yourself to the wrong person and figure it's your last chance for love, and when your inner compass is too weak to tell you to move on. Some women give up hope and live solitary lives, having spent all their emotional energy on too many dead-end relationships."

Kelly didn't want that to happen to her. Though she didn't feel very hopeful, she agreed to trust Martha and let time heal the deepest wounds.

Developing the Inner Compass

One night, Kelly was home alone as usual, watching one of her favorite movies, "You've Got Mail." As usual, she cried at the end, moved by the love story as well as sad about her own plight.

Kelly reviewed the movie in her mind, searching for some truth about her own life, wondering why she couldn't be pursued by a handsome good guy. She couldn't resist thinking *why not me? What's wrong with me, anyway?*

It's no use, thought Kelly despairingly. *According to Martha, there are no magic endings, but that's what I've always hoped for! What is there to look forward to if not that?*

She fell into bed and woke hours later to the sound of her own sobbing, feeling an almost unbearable grief. As she lay there, Kelly felt something inside her break. Something slipped away forever. Perhaps it was her need for magical endings. Maybe it was the childish longings that no longer served her.

The tears stopped. Kelly felt quiet and peaceful, her mind at rest. One question popped into her head: *Why am I here?* She let the question float around, for once not grasping at an immediate answer.

Though she'd grown up attending, Kelly hadn't liked the rigidity of her childhood religion. Her belief in God remained yet she hadn't incorporated that belief into her daily life in a long time. But tonight she felt God's love surrounding her, protecting her. She felt genuinely safe, for the first time ever. Sleepy, she drifted off, leaving her questions to God to solve.

The next morning, Kelly found herself writing in her journal about her experience the night before. Suddenly, she had an insight. *Part of my inner compass*, she thought, *is my spiritual center. That's what I'm missing in my life. That's what I need to develop.*

Kelly's excitement built. For the first time in weeks, she felt peaceful and content, even though she was alone and had no relationship.

The next few days brought waves of insight, as if a dam had broken inside her, and the truth of her life spilled out. With blinding clarity, she saw her terrible choices in men, her huge errors in judgment.

Kelly acknowledged that sex played a huge role in her choices. She confronted the part of her that wanted sexual intimacy with a man, with or without the bonds of commitment. The truth was that it felt only momentarily good.

> *Tip:* "Don't demonize the men in your past. Instead, focus on coming to terms with what you're addicted to that leads to poor relationship choices."

Every time she'd run in the front door of a relationship declaring that she didn't need a commitment, she'd crawled out the back door wounded and bleeding. She just wasn't wired to give herself away sexually without wanting and expecting more.

Kelly sorted through the subject of commitment, realizing that she had no idea what it was like to have real devotion from a man. Part of Kelly was angry with the men in her past. They'd swooped into her life with a few empty promises and then carelessly danced away. She saw clearly the lack of responsibility, the sheer lack of heart. She shared this with Martha.

"Kelly, it's good that you're looking at the issue of character and integrity when it comes to men. But don't go overboard and 'demonize' the men in your past. A more valuable step is for you to come to terms with *your* part in that dance. *What is it that you're addicted to that leads to poor relationship choices?*"

Kelly's brain twisted into a wad of confusion. What did that mean? *Addicted?* She definitely wasn't an addict, though maybe she'd dated a couple of them.

The next morning, she wrote in her journal, asking the question fifteen different ways: *what am I addicted to?* Nothing came back.

In frustration, she closed her journal, closed her eyes, and let her thoughts drift back to the beginning of her relationship with Kevin.

Though it hurt, she forced herself to recall their first week together. She remembered the electric charge of his skin when they kissed and touched. That hadn't faded over the next couple of weeks; in fact, it had intensified. Kelly wondered if sexual and emotional intensity had something to do with addiction.

"Some people never get past the yearning for the early, *enchantment stage* of a relationship," said Martha. "Hooked on excitement, they feel compelled to sabotage or leave relationships once they move into the potentially boring stage of everyday life together. They never learn how to keep a relationship fresh through authentic communication and a focus on what's right between you. It's all about the thrill or lack thereof, not real love.

"The more you hook up with emotionally unavailable people, the more intense this phenomenon. Not seeing your partner in a day-to-day context, always in the drama of attachment vs. withdrawal, you stay locked into the earliest stage of intensity. You have emotional highs and lows but no real equilibrium.

"In healthy relationships," Martha explained, "with commitment and day-to-day familiarity the initial intensity drops. Over time, committed couples settle into a deeper kind of love centered on devotion, not just chemistry. The physical attraction is still there, but it's secondary to the warmth of emotional attachment and bonding."

Breaking the Addiction to Thrills

Kelly resolved to acknowledge the truth about herself, which Martha insisted was the first step in releasing any kind of addictive behavior. She confronted her dark side: *needing* to be loved so much that regardless of the package it arrived in, she grabbed it with both hands. She saw how she'd compromised her own well being, plunging ahead carelessly for the thrill of immediate gratification. Paradoxically, getting what she'd wanted in the moment had cost her what she'd wanted in the long run. The result: *a chain of settle for relationships.*

Kelly admitted she craved excitement. She'd always had an aversion to anything that even remotely resembled the "Steady Eddie" type of guy. Sprinkled in between her "bad boy" relationships there'd been a few "nice guys" who'd bored her silly. Those she had no trouble saying "no" to.

Kelly remembered something Martha had said recently when she'd declared her desire for real commitment in a relationship. "What are you willing to give up in order to attract real commitment?" It didn't make sense at the time, but now it did. *One thing I have to give up is my addiction to emotional thrills. Yuck. How could something so wrong be so appealing?* Kelly thought. Martha encouraged her to feel the reverse—to be *attracted to emotionally available* men and *repulsed by the opposite.* "Put that in your vision and intentions, Kelly, to be attracted to emotionally available men."

Martha's Story

At their next face to face, Kelly expressed her overall despair with her life: the bad decisions of the past, the mess she'd stepped into with Kevin, and her lack of confidence that she could create a good outcome. She sighed and lapsed into silence. After a while, Kelly looked up at Martha, curiosity replacing her self-absorption.

"What about you, Martha? Are you happily married? I don't know anything about you."

Martha smiled. "I'm blessed with a wonderful man whose love I draw upon every day."

"How did you get where you are today, Martha? What motivates you to help women like me?"

Martha smiled. "You're right, Kelly, you deserve to hear my story." She paused for a moment as if to gather her thoughts. When she spoke, her voice was low and soft. Emotion hovered in the background. Kelly listened, spellbound.

✳ ✳ ✳

Martha was barely nineteen when she met Rick. Young and full of naïve optimism about love, she picked a guy who drank too much and had no ambition. While charming and loads of fun in the beginning, it didn't take long for his behavior to change to something darker. He had difficulty keeping a job because his superiors were all "idiots." He spent more time out with his buddies drinking than he did at home with Martha.

Martha struggled to make her marriage work but found that having any kind of meaningful conversation with Rick was impossible. Little by little, she surrendered her own personal esteem in the effort to shore up Rick's. Meanwhile, she worked full time and went to school at night so that she could have a good career, knowing that she was the one who would support them financially. Then, the unexpected news: Martha was pregnant.

To Martha's disappointment, Rick expressed more dismay than joy. By the time Shelley was born, she knew that she had made a terrible mistake. Rick was drunk most of the time and she became fearful that he would do something to hurt the baby while she was at school or work. Finally, she divorced him, resolving to be a good single Mom and do the best she could. Rick easily gave up parental rights in exchange for not paying child support. Martha was relieved that he wouldn't be involved in Shelley's life. She thought she was out of the woods, but her attraction to the wrong kind of guy did not die. It simply went dormant for a few years while Martha struggled to finish school and get her career going.

"When Shelley was five, my career took off. I landed a great job with a start-up company and bought a nice home for the first time. I felt like I'd sacrificed my personal life for years for school, work, and being a Mom. It was like a dam burst inside. I cut loose. The good girl I'd always been disappeared and the party girl took over." Martha sounded matter of fact, but Kelly detected a note of chagrin in her voice.

In the nineteen seventies, disco dancing and free love were in; traditional values were out. She went out at night with girl friends, drinking and dancing, leaving Shelley with a nanny. The freewheeling spirit that she longed to express came to the forefront.

Martha's chooser was broken, but she pushed aside her awareness of that. She had one relationship after another with men who were unwilling to commit. She slept with them, traveled with them, broke up their marriages, and got her heart broken by them. She longed to find that "perfect mate" who would love and cherish her, but every man she chose believing he could be *"the one"* turned out to be a huge disappointment. Meanwhile, her baby was growing up quickly and she was missing most of it. Still, Shelley was the one bright and perfect spot in her life.

"Shelley had a sparkling personality and was always laughing. She drew pictures for me and babbled about anything and everything. At night, she cried sometimes, usually as I was leaving to go out."

Martha's eyes brimmed and her voice caught. Her chin trembled. After a few moments, she continued in a tight voice.

"Looking back, I know I did the wrong things. I emotionally abandoned my daughter to satisfy my own unmet emotional needs. And the irony is that the more I tried to meet those needs with the men I dated, the emptier I felt. There was Tom, who moved in when Shelley was ten. I kicked him out after a disastrous year. Then there was Peter who I married after only two months, but divorced quickly when I discovered he'd been seeing his ex. I hate to admit this, but by age thirteen, Shelley had seen a parade of men in and out of my life—and hers.

"I stopped dating when Shelley was fourteen because I finally realized what a bad example I was setting for my daughter. I poured myself into trying to help her but it was already too late.

"I realize now that I enabled Shelley to do all the wrong things. Shelley became a little bohemian. She refused to go to college and wanted to be an actress. I gave her money so she could follow her passion, but she turned around and gave it to her drug-dealing boyfriend. Shelley's self-esteem was terribly low and I felt guilty and responsible for it. Instead of helping her face it and grow up, I cushioned her."

Shelley's life spiraled downward. She married her drug addict boyfriend who became increasingly violent. Lacking the emotional strength to walk away, Shelley stayed, convinced she could fix it by doing the right things so he wouldn't get angry.

"I knew something was wrong but wasn't sure what. Shelley insisted everything was okay at home, but I knew something was off. My laughing, bubbly daughter turned into a depressed, timid, nervous woman.

"I gave her money and offered to help, but she accused me of trying to ruin her marriage like I'd ruined my own. I found out later that the violence had been escalating. Shelley was trying to be a responsible adult but in all the wrong ways. She wanted to be independent from me, but in striving for that she trapped herself in a terrible situation."

Martha stopped at that point and closed her eyes, pain etching her lovely features. She would remember every detail of what happened next for the rest of her life. It was burned into her brain.

Martha called her daughter's house one day, surprised to hear her son-in-law Bobby's voice. "She's out," was all he said, and hung up. She called every day for a week, getting the same answer. Finally, alarmed and concerned for her daughter's safety, she called the police and convinced them to go with her to Shelley's house to question her husband. Bobby answered the door in a drugged stupor. He was belligerent with the police, who handcuffed him and put him in the squad car. Martha and the officers went into the house and found the most unimaginable scene of horror.

"Bobby had killed Shelley during a drug-induced rage. When she was autopsied, we discovered her pregnancy. Bobby was eventually convicted and sentenced to life in prison.

"I thought the grief would kill me. I couldn't face my friends. I even considered suicide. I'd failed the one person I loved the most."

Kelly wiped her eyes as she listened, picturing beautiful, laughing Shelley, the baby she'd never had, and the loss of her young life in such a tragic and senseless way. Martha dabbed her eyes with a napkin. Telling the story was painful every single time.

After months of depression, she woke up one day and confronted the selfishness of her behavior. In a moment of clarity, she saw that she had to emerge from her prison of self-punishment and re-enter life. The best way to honor her daughter would be to help others avoid a similar fate.

Martha returned to school to fulfill her mission. She studied sociology, psychology, world religion, and everything she could get her hands on about the history of women's rights. She resolved to devote the rest of her life helping young women re-build their self-esteem, establish fulfilling careers and a sense of purpose, and choose men wisely.

"I was lucky enough to cash out of my business with more money than I could possibly spend. I used most of it to establish a group home for displaced teenage girls, naming it Shelley's Place. The girls, neglected or abused in their prior homes, were given a stable environment, support for staying in school, and counseling. With a safe place to live and an emphasis on education, almost all of the girls went on to college and careers. Instead of falling through the cracks in society, they blossomed into productive women with promising futures.

"When we founded the group home, we set out to do a great deal more than just provide food and shelter, more than standard foster care. We educated these young women in every part of life, including their future relationships with men. We hired professionals, created programs to help them boost their self-esteem and look at the consequences of their life choices. We made sure that relationships with boys and how to manage them were a huge topic of discussion."

Martha stopped, her voice faltering.

"In the early months, rage was a big factor. I was so angry that there were times I fantasized about killing Bobby. I knew I couldn't bring Shelley back or change the past. The only way I could overcome the unending pain of losing her was to channel those feelings into helping the girls."

Kelly realized Martha was more than the soft and enlightened mentor Kelly knew. She was emotional like anyone else; she could be sad, depressed, and even furious.

"We taught them the value of education in that it gave them choices. We encouraged abstinence and gave them the emotional tools to do so, showing them what was at stake: not just pregnancy but the damaged self-esteem from sleeping with boys who are too young to commit and almost certain to abandon them.

"We helped them focus on discovering and using their own special gifts and talents, to develop a sense of accomplishment and worth. The program really works, Kelly. The home is so successful that we've opened branches in two other major cities. Now, I spend most of my time fund-raising for the three group homes."

Martha paused before continuing.

"One night at a fund-raiser for Shelley's Place, I met John. He was a widower whose wife had died of cancer a couple of years earlier. He was so nice, calling me and asking me out. At first, I pushed him away. I hadn't dated in years and wasn't sure that it was possible for me to make a good choice. Honestly, I didn't believe I deserved to be loved." Martha's clear eyes shone with the memories of her early days with John.

"But he was persistent, and gradually I realized that holding back on having a good, loving relationship was contrary to the natural flow of life. It wasn't about whether or not I deserved it. It was about honoring life, healing, and moving forward. I also realized that learning how to have a healthy relationship was part of my mission, an integral part of it. So I dated John and we stumbled around, learned a lot, and found our way to a deep and lasting love. It hardly seems possible, but we love each other more today than ever."

One day, Martha had been approached by a young woman much like Kelly who'd asked Martha to mentor her. Martha had agreed with the stipulation that if it worked she would assist with the group home as payment for the program. So far, she'd mentored six young women, all of whom remained involved in the mission. "And the rest," she concluded, "you know. I take on clients like you so I can keep the mission going and leave a legacy."

Kelly's Commitment

Over the next few days, Kelly reflected. She realized that she'd looked at her situation from entirely the wrong perspective.

I've been so self-absorbed, she thought. *I've anguished over these guys who probably don't give me a second thought, and meanwhile, other people are faced with truly life-and-death situations. Life*, she thought, *is so fragile. So impossibly short.*

She called Martha to share her epiphany. "I've spent years focusing on the wrong things," she said, "on my feelings, my desire for instant gratification, my childish wish for a man to come along and sweep me off my feet, make up for every loss.

"Well, no more! *Life is too short* to waste my heart and energy like that." She took a deep breath, feeling her anger rise.

"Martha, I've had it. I'm done, *really done* with non-intentional, emotionally unavailable men. I'm through with settling for these dead-end, draining relationships.

"I'm ready to give up my addiction to excitement when it comes to men. I see now that the bigger the initial thrill, the greater the damage at the end. There's something in me that's drawn to guys who are bound to break my heart. I'm ready to change that, *no matter what I have to do or how long it takes. I would rather be single for the rest of my life than set myself up to get hurt like this again.* If I spend a lot of Saturday nights alone, so be it! I'm in no hurry."

Martha seemed truly impressed. "That's very powerful, Kelly."

"But my question is this: am I going too far the other way, putting up a wall? Am I setting myself up to be alone?"

> *In order for you to have a strong 'yes,' you must first develop a strong 'no.' The biggest commitment you need to make is to your own well-being.*

"What do *you* think? What do you have to lose by drawing a line in the sand and declaring that you'll no longer compromise your values?"

Kelly considered that. "A few dates maybe. But frankly, saying yes too quickly hasn't worked. Maybe I need to learn how to say no a few times. This is such a brain twister—I'm getting a headache." She tacked on the last comment half jokingly.

"Don't analyze it too much, Kelly. I'll leave you with this thought. Someone once told me: *In order for you to have a strong 'yes,' you must develop a strong 'no.'* The biggest commitment you need to make is the commitment to your own well being."

Kelly felt something well up inside—an indescribable feeling, poignant and full. "That's it! That's what I've been trying to say. I feel *totally committed to taking excellent care of myself emotionally.* I'm the ultimate health food, working out, vitamin-taking girl, but I completely overlooked my health when it came to men! Until now."

Kelly's voice softened. "That *desperate to be loved* feeling is going away, Martha. What's growing in its place is this love for me, this commitment to taking care of me first and foremost. And it doesn't feel selfish the way I thought it would. It feels natural and right. I feel like I now have so much more to offer in a relationship."

The Sixth Temptation:

Aiming for the Fairy Tale

Chapter Six

Kelly gradually moved on with her life, reconnecting with friends, having dinner, catching a movie.

She refrained from jumping back into the dating scene. For the first time ever, she was in no rush to date someone new, determined to break her pattern of serial monogamy.

Martha reminded her, "This is the best time to really zero in on the most important things you need to know and the most vital steps you need to take going forward. Can you guess why this is good timing?"

Kelly laughed. "I suppose because I don't seem to use my brain very well once I get attached to someone."

"Exactly. Most of us stop learning when we meet someone we're attracted to, so while you're in between relationships, we'll focus on what you need to know before you resume dating."

Coaching Steps: Undoing Myths and Faulty Thinking

At their next meeting, Kelly arrived armed with spiral notebook and pen, ready to learn. It was early January and the timing was perfect for turning the page to a new chapter of life.

"What we're going to do is create a powerful vision for your life and relationships going forward. Having a clear, compelling vision for your ideal relationship enables you to achieve it. But first, we need to do serious damage to some myths and erroneous ways of thinking that in the past have prevented you from getting what you really want. Thoughts held as beliefs guide your choices, and we're going to expose the ones that don't work, then create some completely new ones so that your choices are based on the things that really count in good relationships.

The Problem with Dating

"Dating, once called courting, was historically governed by strict social rules and conducted under the watchful eye of parents who sought to protect young people from succumbing to raging hormones and making poor choices. All that disappeared a few decades ago. Now, you're on your own. Dating as we know it today is pretty much a free-for-all, with no guidelines unless you create them for yourself. Meanwhile, you're constantly tempted to make serious mistakes that cost you in time and heartache. Why? Because *spending time alone with someone you're attracted to stirs up your emotions and your hormones,* and most of us don't handle that well."

Martha paused, then asked, "Let's begin with you; what are *your* temptations, Kelly?"

Kelly thought about it for a couple of minutes. "I'm tempted to sleep with a guy when there's a lot of chemistry and I think we're heading towards a commitment."

"Okay, let's say that you give in to that temptation and sleep with a guy too soon. What happens next?"

"I fall in love too soon. I devote myself to him. I don't stop to assess whether he's right for me, I just dive in deeper." Kelly frowned, embarrassed by her past behavior.

"Great, Kelly, you just identified several of the main issues. Recall the first few temptations: denial of your true wishes, leaving integrity out of the picture, choosing high-risk relationships and sacrificing self-care to do so, all of which lead you down the path to settling for less. Not to mention going for those wounded guys! These temptations make up a vicious cycle of behavior: one leads to the next and so on. Can you see that, Kelly?"

Kelly grimaced. "Yes, I can. I always *think* I'm getting someone really wonderful but I'm wrong every time. How can that be?"

"Good question. Remember the first time we met and I asked you what you wanted?"

"Yes. What a confusing conversation that was!"

Martha smiled. "I'm sure it was, and rightfully so. Defining what you really want is one of the most challenging parts of the process. So, tell me, what do you look for in a guy?"

Kelly thought for a moment, then shared the criteria that she'd used in the past to judge guys for dating material: College educated, sophisticated, likes the arts, intelligent, adventurous, good looking, sexy, physically fit, and financially successful.

"So let me get this straight. You carefully thought it out and chose Kevin because married men are a good bargain? They make the cut on your list?"

"No! It just happened," Kelly protested defensively.

"Nothing over which you have direct control 'just happens.' You *do* have control over who you go out with; therefore, you choose all of your relationships."

"I suppose you're right. It's hard to admit, but it's true," Kelly sighed. "I did choose Kevin."

"Why? What was it that drew you in?"

"He was so cute and charming and romantic," Kelly admitted. "He made me feel special."

"So you chose him because hormones, emotions, and chemistry ruled the day," Martha stated flatly. She softened her voice. "*Where are your value statements?*"

Kelly dropped her eyes, feeling defeated. "I guess it never really occurred to me to look at my values when I chose a man."

"It's a big step to admit that. Most women choose their next dating partner based solely on attraction; whatever lists they have go flying out the window as soon as a cute guy saunters up and shows a little interest. Then there's the woman who finds a guy who meets the list, but there's no chemistry. She's tired of looking, so she dates him hoping it will magically transform into a good relationship. Women who are single a long time often flip-flop between one dynamic and the other: first the high-chemistry, high risk relationship, then the no-chemistry, boring one. Neither works.

"Speaking of high-chemistry, high-risk relationships: where do we see lots of examples of them?"

> *"It's not in our best interest to have multiple, intense romances that go nowhere. The more a woman engages in risky behavior—opening wide in every way with guys she barely knows or men of poor character—the less she's able to be vulnerable in the right way with the right guy."*

"I see it all the time in the movies and on television."

"That's right—the glamorous 'Sex and the City' lifestyle that we try to emulate. We've accepted that it's okay to give ourselves away to men with no thought of the future or our basic compatibility, let alone commitment. Women on television and in the movies do it and end up with the guy, so we believe it will work for us. Instead of using a smart strategy, we rely on hormones and chance. Making one stupid mistake after another eventually leads to the miracle: the great guy who sweeps us out of the mess of our personal lives and makes us happy."

Martha let that sink in for a moment before continuing. "*It's not in our best interest to have multiple, intense romances with men that go nowhere, Kelly.* It takes months, sometimes years, to recover from each one.

"Paradoxically, the more a woman engages in risky behavior—opening wide in every way with guys she barely knows or men of poor character—the less she's able to be vulnerable in the right way with the right guy. Over time, our hearts close. We become cynical, jaded. Our goal instead is *smart dating*: choosing loving men of good character who are emotionally available."

Smart Dating: No More Crystal Balls

"But how do you learn to choose better? How do I know in advance if I've found a good guy or not, Martha? I choose who to go out with, sure, but I can't predict their character. I don't have a crystal ball!"

"Exactly! *So why sleep with a guy and open your heart to him, when you don't know him or his true character or intentions?* Trying to analyze him and predict the future doesn't work. Forget crystal balls and psychics.

"Let's say you meet a guy, like him, he fits your basic list. But it takes time to uncover someone's true character, so you *pace* the relationship so you can both feel very sure of your choice down the road.

"If he's the kind of guy with no intentions toward real commitment, how patient is he likely to be once he realizes you're not going to sleep with him, that you're going to gradually explore the possibility of a future together, and furthermore, you're marriage minded?"

> *"The most powerful tool you have is adherence to a dating process that weeds out men who are emotionally unavailable, incompatible, or of questionable character."*

"Not at all! The guys I've dated would pretty much hit the road at that point."

"Right. *The most powerful tool you have is adherence to a dating process* that weeds out men who are emotionally unavailable, incompatible, or of questionable character. It's the *process* that makes the difference, Kelly, not some magic foresight that enables you to predict the future. Without it, you're trapped in a cycle of *serial monogamy*—moving impulsively from one relationship to the next without any real learning or growth. The first step in the process is clearly defining what you're looking for."

Someday My Prince Will Come… And Other Unlikely Fairy Tales

Martha introduced the **Sixth Temptation:** *aiming for the fairy tale* picture of what you want rather than the real thing. "Think of it like a target. Instead of aiming for a guy who's capable of love and devotion, who shares your values and wants the same things, you aim for the guy who makes a big impression when he walks into the room. He's hot and successful, and all the women want his attention. He makes your heart race like a hero from a good romance novel.

"Next thing you know, he's swept you off your feet and into bed, and you're dreaming of an elaborate proposal while vacationing in

Tuscany complete with a diamond big enough to make your friends' eyes pop out. In reality, you couldn't be more off target."

"But what if the right guy is *all* of those things?" Kelly asked. "What if he's loving, devoted, shares my values, and also happens to be successful and sexy? Why can't I find all that wrapped up in one guy?"

"It's possible, Kelly. But you'll never be able to control that kind of outcome because *you're aiming for the wrong things*. Good relationships happen by aiming for the *right* things, and trusting that when you hit that bulls-eye, he's right for you in every way, even if he's not the best-looking or richest guy in town."

Kelly sighed. "I don't get it. It seems like I'm settling if I don't aim for the guy who has it all."

Martha smiled. "If you don't want to settle, we have to start by articulating what you want. And if he's right for you, you'll be attracted to him, and you'll know it. Can you trust me when I say that there are plenty of guys out there that you can feel that way about?"

"I'll try."

The Right Target:
Emotional Availability and Matching Values

"Good. Now, let's look at emotional availability. How do you define it and how important is that to you?"

Kelly thought for a minute or so. "It's very important. If he's emotionally available, then he's not with anyone else. Or married," she added sheepishly.

"Okay. Let's say he's not with anyone else or married, does that automatically mean he's emotionally available?"

"No. He could have other issues, baggage from past relationships, or an addiction problem. Then there's the geographical barrier—I don't think I'd be happy dating someone long distance."

"That's right. There are many ways that a guy may be emotionally unavailable. We'll come back to how you can tell if he is in a minute. Now, I want you to think about values. How important is it to you that the man you spend your life with shares your values?"

"It's hugely important. I can't imagine settling for any less."

"How can you tell if a guy shares your values? What about a spiritual connection? Don't answer that part yet—put it in the bucket with how to know about his emotional availability."

Tip: "Focus on the relationship and character values that matter to you. Describing a person locks you into a mind-set that can cause you to miss Mr. Right because you are focused on the skin-deep things that don't count in the long run."

Martha asked her to write down her core values in words and phrases. She quickly wrote a list of things such as love of family, integrity, charity, and kindness. She added: adventurous, passion for life, commitment to health, and desire for learning and growth, among others.

Then Martha asked her to write a list of core values regarding the *attributes of a relationship* that she wanted and needed. Kelly composed another list that included: open, honest communication, affection, good sexual connection, respect, consideration, and kindness.

"Notice that I'm not asking you to write down descriptors of the guy, such as tall, athletic, in shape, nice hair and eyes, good dancer, etc. *Describing a person* locks you into a mind-set that can cause you to miss Mr. Right. It focuses you on the skin-deep things that don't count in the long run. Instead, I want you to focus on the relationship and character values that matter and let the process that I'll teach you draw in the right person."

Martha instructed her to write down her non-negotiables: the things that she could *not live without* in a relationship and the things that she could *not live with*. Kelly wrote a short list that included: non-smoker, no drugs, light alcohol, wants kids, takes care of his health, and shares my spiritual beliefs.

By the time she finished, Kelly felt mentally exhausted. They took a break, walking around for a while, checking out some of the boutiques in the Uptown area. They chose a small table at a cozy wine bar and each ordered a glass.

Zeroing in on the Target

Martha began. "Let's return to the issue of character, Kelly. How do you define good character in a man? What do you look for?"

"I haven't thought much about it before. I just assumed that a guy had good character if we hit it off and if he didn't do anything obvious to make me think differently. That sounds lame, doesn't it?"

"No, it sounds very typical. Historically, women were attracted to the physically strongest male because they offered protection in a dangerous world. Women are still susceptible to that imagery when choosing a mate. In modern times, it also translates to seeking the guy with the most money because money equals power. However, *neither one of these is the real target.*

"Money comes and goes. Later in life, physical strength wanes, a person can get sick. What really counts through all of life is *strength of character.* How do you measure strength of character? Bottom line: through behavior. That means that he does the right things and he doesn't do the wrong things. I'm talking about the *important* things.

"In dating, we measure a guy's character by noticing the little things: he shows up when he says he will; he fulfills his commitments; he keeps his word. He respects your boundaries, doesn't push you into anything that makes you uncomfortable. You can count on him, more not less as time goes on. His friends, business associates, and family respect him. He has relationships in his past, but no trail of destruction. Rather, the women in his past still like him and see him as a good guy. It is not in his nature to be deceitful or cruel. He's honest. What you *really* look for," Martha concluded, "is that kind of strength of character."

Then she asked, "So, how do you suppose you might discern a man's true character?"

"I'm not at all sure how to do that." Kelly reflected while Martha waited. "I guess one way is to ask him."

"Okay. How would you pose the question?"

"Well, I'd start with sharing my values and then ask him how he feels about that."

"Now, let's say you did that and he pretty much mirrored back what you shared. What have you learned?"

Kelly felt confused again. "Um, I guess not a whole lot," she paused then laughed, "except that he's good at saying what I want to hear!"

"That's right. Most women spend the first couple of dates going over their lists and checking off items as a match just because a guy successfully echoes her sentiments. While it's true that some guys really mean what they're saying, I'm sure you know that a lot of guys don't. They know they need to say the right things in order to get another date, so they do, but it doesn't mean that it's coming from the heart."

"So what else can I do? I guess I can Google him, make sure he doesn't have a criminal record."

"That wouldn't hurt," Martha acknowledged. "However, there's something else you can do. First, you can practice *pacing*. While you're doing that, you can interview him."

Interviewing for Mr. Right

"Interview him?" Kelly was really puzzled now. "What does that mean?"

"*The best predictor of future behavior is past behavior.* So if you meet a guy and you find out that he always leaves relationships, what does that tell you he's likely to do with you? Or, what if you find out that he's never made a commitment to a woman? What does that kind of information tell you?"

Feeling chagrined, Kelly answered off the top of her head, "In the past, it told me that I had a great project ahead of me!"

Martha laughed. "And now?"

"Looking back, I can see that the way he acted with the last woman was basically the same with me."

"Right; *he is who he is.* Your job isn't to try to change him—it's frustrating for you and for him and it

"Behavior is the true determinant of a person's strength of character, and the best indicator of future behavior is past behavior - how he's treated women in the past."

> *"Your job isn't to change him, but rather to see exactly who the person is in front of you."*

doesn't work. Rather, your job is to *see exactly who the person is in front of you.* Then you can make a fully informed decision about getting closer and exploring a future together. So, how do you discern those things up front?"

"I guess I need to ask questions about his past. But that seems so intrusive! Won't a guy clam up if I drill him about his past? Isn't that personal and sensitive information?"

"What could be more personal or sensitive than emotional and sexual intimacy, falling in love? Dating is very personal! The purpose of dating is not to decide what to order for dinner—it's to make *life-altering decisions* about who to share your life with, make babies with. Of course it's personal!

"In order to discern who's right for you, you have to crack open some eggs. You have every right to ask those questions, just as he has the right to query you about your past."

Kelly's face fell at that thought. "Great," she mumbled. "I guess I'm supposed to tell every guy I go out with that I slept with a married man."

"No, you don't tell every guy you go out with. You share it with someone special in the spirit of revealing who you are through the path of your life, your choices then and your choices now.

"Most people avoid discussing personal information about their past with people they date. But think of it this way. If someone held back *significant information* about his past, how do you imagine you'd feel finding out after you married him?"

"Betrayed! Especially if that information told me that he's not safe."

"It works both ways, Kelly. He has the right to know your true character as well."

Kelly wrote furiously, but paused as another question occurred to her. "What about personal growth, Martha? Don't you believe that people can change? Couldn't a guy have poor relationships in his past and change for the better?"

"What do *you* think?"

"I believe people can change. I'm changing; I feel it. My attitudes and beliefs are changing almost daily since we started working together."

"I agree with you—people change. You chose to go into this program for that specific purpose, and you had some issues that didn't bode well for the next guy. The thing is, people change because *they choose it*, and they do so for *internal* reasons, not external ones. If a guy changes and grows, it's not because he hooks up with you and you demand it. Women tend to believe that love changes men, and let's face it: Hollywood has consistently reinforced that myth.

"People change because their lives have become unmanageable in some way and they have the guts to admit it and do something about it. They change for themselves, not because they want to prove something to another person. That kind of change is fleeting, not sustainable over time.

"The right guy for you may be someone who went through some major changes, but don't kid yourself—if he's not in a good place in his life when you meet him, it won't be good for you. Remember, love is about *acceptance*—finding someone you can love for exactly who he is when you meet him."

"Okay, I think I get it. So what questions should I ask when I interview him?"

Martha covered the questions while Kelly took notes. Kelly tried to picture herself on a date asking them and realized that she had some work to do to feel confident enough to follow through with this part of her homework. *This is hard*, she thought. At the same time, she saw the potential to save herself tons of heartache.

It's Really a Marathon

"Now I want to talk about pacing. Take a guess about what that means."

"Well, I suppose it means taking your time, going slowly in a relationship. But I've heard people use that term a lot and it seems like the ones who say they're going slow are the ones who get married three months after they meet. What's that about?"

"Great question. *Going slow* is an often misused phrase in dating. Usually it means there's good reason to be cautious, they see the red flags, but they FEEL in love. What they SAY is 'we're going slowly' but what they DO is sleep together, spend all their time together, and fantasize about their future together. They marry quickly and defend it by saying that they KNEW it was the right thing to do. Quick marriages have a higher probability of divorce for the simple reason that people in that situation *don't know what they're choosing.* They don't have enough history together. Later, when they find out who the real person is, there's usually a huge let down.

"Our personalities are too layered to really know a person in three or six or even nine months of dating. The top, most visible layer is the social mask that we wear every day. Underneath that are the more vulnerable parts: our fears, insecurities, the things that tick us off, and so on. It takes time to uncover those parts; we don't really know a person until we see him exposed and vulnerable. It's at our worst: angry, hurt, and fearful, that our true character emerges.

"We rush into marriage because people, especially women, are in love with the *idea* of being in love, with the romantic pictures in their minds of their wedding day. Our culture *worships* the 'in love' stage of a relationship and shuns the day-to-day work of sustaining a marriage over decades through good and bad times.

"Life is full of challenges: heartache, disappointment, and loss. What matters is *how we respond* to those challenges. Don't you want to have some idea of how the man you choose responds to life's challenges?

"That's what dating is really for, Kelly. It's about knowing someone long enough for the mask to fall away. It's about seeing each other at our best and at our worst. That takes pacing, and pacing is not at all the same as going slow the way most people do it. That's why I use a totally different term, so that you can easily see the distinction.

No More Sprinting: Winning the Marathon

"**Pacing** is putting off intimacy for a lengthy period of time while you get to know each other. You see each other infrequently and for short dates at first, gradually increasing frequency and length of dates over time, refraining from sex for months, or even waiting until after marriage, until your commitment is solid."

"I bet a lot of guys would be put off by this pacing idea."

"What kind of guys?"

"The guys who want a good time with no strings attached." Kelly thought a bit more and added, "Also, the insecure guys who can't stand not having a woman fall all over them."

> *Tip:* "Pace your relationships by putting off intimacy while you get to know each other. Begin with short, infrequent dates and gradually increase frequency and length of dates over time. Refrain from sex until your commitment is solid."

"Bottom line, Kelly: guys who can't respect pacing are fundamentally insecure, and insecure men don't make good husbands. Insecurity is another word for fear, and a fear-based marriage is a battlefield.

"All of us struggle to some extent with fear—we dread rejection, loss, and abandonment. But, when we're healthy, we're dominated by love and we believe good things will happen. This makes us more centered on giving to others than on protecting ourselves, which makes us good mates.

"An emotionally secure man does that naturally. He assumes that good things will happen, he trusts you, and he puts most of his focus on making you, the woman he adores, happy."

Kelly sat and listened, visualizing what Martha was talking about. She took a deep breath, let it out slowly, and blinked back tears. She felt deeply sad that she hadn't experienced anything like that in any of her relationships. Part of her wondered if it was possible; another part of her desperately hoped it was.

That evening, Kelly quietly reflected over a glass of Cabernet. Though her past was littered with men she'd loved but who were incapable of devotion, she still felt hopeful about her future. *I can do this*, she told herself silently. *I can change this pattern. I will change*, she declared. *I am changing.*

The Seventh Temptation:

Getting Sexual Too Soon

Chapter Seven

The next day, Kelly asked lots of questions, trying to understand how to pace a relationship. Martha assured her that practice would make it all clear. "The real test," Martha said, "is following through behaviorally, especially when you're tempted. It's all about adhering to your commitment to self."

"If you feel special already, you're not drawn to emotionally unavailable men because you recognize that he can't reflect what *you feel inside* about yourself."

They took a break, walking through one of the nicer of Dallas' many malls, until they found a quiet restaurant for a late lunch. Martha quickly jumped into a new topic. "Let's talk about sex and emotions, Kelly. When a woman gives herself away too quickly, she dooms herself to emotional neediness. He makes a few commitment noises, offers some crumbs of affection, and she thinks he's falling in love. She has sex with him, opens her heart, and thinks they're a couple. She's totally devoted and planning their future, but *he's still checking her out.*

"Loving him unconditionally while he's still deciding creates emotional imbalance. She feels insecure because his signals tell her that he's not entirely on board with this glorious future that she's mapped out.

"She acts needy because she's questioning his feelings for her. She tries to speed things up so that she can find an emotionally secure place with him. He reacts by pulling away which leads to more neediness!

"Pacing resolves these issues up front by helping you avoid the **Seventh Temptation:** *getting sexual too soon.* You pace a relationship by holding back your heart and your sexuality long enough for the relationship to balance naturally. Does this make sense so far?"

"I guess, but how does this fit in with the sexual revolution? You grew up then. Help me understand it."

"Good question. The nineteen sixties may have appeared to be a sexual revolution for women, but in reality it was the beginning of the playboy mentality that persists today. Guys believe that having sex with women without loving them or making a real commitment is okay, that there are no consequences for such behavior. We as women have colluded by pretending it doesn't matter to us if we have sex without commitment.

"Women have to shift the tide by acknowledging that this big social experiment, the so-called free love movement, betrayed us. It didn't give us better, more loving, relationships. It merely cheapened the ultimate expression of intimacy between men and women, made it no more special than buying a new pair of shoes. It also put us at great emotional, psychological, and even physical risk.

Sex, Love, and Emotions

"We have to break the cycle of the first temptation: denying our true wishes for a loving relationship. We're not okay with sex without commitment, not with the men we really want. Do women have sex with men that they *don't* want a commitment from? Of course! But that's just giving back what hurt us before—we're using men to gratify our needs at their expense. Trading hurts doesn't build a healthy relationship dynamic between men and women.

"Pacing a relationship means taking sex off the table for a considerable period of time while you focus on really getting to know someone, without a false sense of urgency or emotional imbalance. In most cases, dating for a period of one year before

> *"Pacing a relationship means taking sex off the table for a considerable period of time while you focus on really getting to know someone, without the false sense of urgency or emotional imbalance that arises from having sex too soon."*

engagement, then a year of engagement without planning the wedding until the last six months, allows time to learn what you need to know to marry someone with confidence."

Kelly's eyes widened. Martha smiled. "This isn't a hard and fast rule, Kelly. It's a guideline. Every couple's timeline to marriage is different. The point is, I want you to seriously consider the power of pacing. Giving up the rush to marriage and putting off sex prevents you from getting attached to the wrong men."

"I get that. But why is it that women have to be guarded about the timing of sex? Why is it that guys can sleep around and not be affected by it? That doesn't seem fair. Are we really so different when it comes to sex?"

Men and Sex: Dessert before Dinner

Martha paused, searching for a good analogy. "Think of it this way, Kelly. Men and sex are like your diet and ice cream. Imagine that you're trying to stay slim. You go out to eat. The first course is butter pecan ice cream—your favorite. You eat it. Now imagine that the second course is grilled salmon and steamed vegetables. How much appetite do you have for the fish and veggies?"

"Not much, obviously!" Kelly said, laughing.

"Sex for men is like the butter pecan ice cream. If you offer him that first, he'll gorge himself on it, and he won't have an appetite for the next course, which is the love and commitment part."

"That sounds like *why buy the cow when you can get the milk for free*! Does that really fit today's relationships?"

"Some things are universally true, Kelly. Men are biologically wired to seek sexual connection. In order for a man to seek love and commitment, he has to develop a certain level of emotional maturity. He has to be ready to focus on the big picture of his life, what he really wants, his values.

"That's one of the reasons why late teen and early twenties marriages fail at a much higher rate than marriages for more mature couples. Teenage and early twenty-something men are very driven by sexual urges. Generally speaking, they're too immature to seek or understand more."

"Okay, I get that. But I'm not dating teenagers. I'm dating guys in their thirties and forties."

"The men you're dating, though older, grew up in a culture that worships sexuality. Young women today overtly advertise their sexuality, dressing provocatively and putting themselves in situations in which hormones rule.

"For women, the butter pecan ice cream is the love and commitment. When we offer sex up front, we're hoping he'll magically fall in love. Sometimes he does, but most of the time he doesn't. The result is rampant confusion for both genders.

"Today, most single men have a history of relationships with women in which they put sex first, working on love and commitment much later. They're primed for that dynamic; they expect it. Even the good guys fall into the trap of putting sex first, and they get burned as well. They're in no position to control pacing."

"So how do I deal with all of this?"

Get Real Honey!

"Well, basically you have to turn the tables on men's expectations. You have to get things in the right order to maximize the chances that love will rule and that sex will happen in the context of a real commitment. I realize it sounds old-fashioned."

"Yes it does, but I hear these stories all the time. I've lived these stories!" Kelly paused and reflected, looking uncertain.

"What is it you're stuck on?"

"I've heard that you should withhold sex from guys until they commit, but I wrote that off as manipulative. I don't want a guy that way—it seems false and insincere."

"You're right, Kelly. If you dress and act provocatively, at the same time withholding sex for the purpose of reeling a guy in, it's manipulative. If you're up front that you want a marriage partner, you're being real, and you're willing to let the chips fall where they may."

"But even marriage-minded guys could be put off if I look too desperate."

> *Desperate pushes people away. Intentional, on the other hand, draws them in.*

"You're right and that's an important distinction. *Desperate* pushes people away. *Intentional,* on the other hand, draws them in. Do you see the difference?"

"I think so. I'm definitely not desperate. I *want* to get married, but I don't *need* it and I don't feel too much urgency about it."

"Good. Getting back to the ice cream and the main course, let's imagine another scenario. You sit down at the restaurant and see butter pecan ice cream on the menu. First you get the fish and veggies, deliciously prepared, all the time eagerly anticipating that butter pecan ice cream! You save plenty of room for it and they bring it out. Do you think you might want to eat it?"

"You bet! And love every bite." Kelly smiled.

"Exactly! Keep in mind *it's the same ice cream.* There's nothing wrong with butter pecan ice cream, just as there's nothing wrong with sex. But the *timing* makes a world of difference to your body, just as the timing of sex makes a world of difference in your relationship."

Martha paused to let it all sink in. "Can you to agree to put off sex with the men you date for a minimum of six months?"

Kelly's jaw dropped. "Six months?! That seems like forever. I don't think I've put it off for six weeks, let alone six months!"

"I promise it will radically change your dating patterns and open you up to new experiences, good ones. It's critical to your success."

"I have to think about this, Martha. What about my sexual needs in the meantime?"

"You have sexual *desires*, not needs. Sex isn't something we *need* like air, food, and water. It's a biological driver and something we enjoy, even crave, in the physical and emotional sense. However, no one ever died from lack of sex. Lots of people live celibate lives, and are quite healthy and vibrant."

"Okay, okay, I get it. I guess I'll have to get a good vibrator!" Kelly said, laughing.

"There's nothing wrong with that!" Martha laughed. "In fact, knowing how to please yourself sexually is important for two reasons.

One, you curb your appetite so that you're less tempted to sleep with guys. Two, you learn your own body so that you can teach your husband how to give you pleasure.

Women and Sex: Love Through the Front Door

"Your temptation to be sexual too soon is mostly driven by the tendency of women to confuse love and sex, aiming for love through the back door of sex.

"The idea that sex and emotions can be divorced within a person's life is pure myth. We're wired to bond, and sex is a powerful bonding mechanism.

"A healthy goal is to bond emotionally, spiritually, and intellectually, and once a real commitment is made, to extend that bonding into a sexual relationship. Does that make sense?"

"Yes, but what about sexual compatibility? What if I do all that bonding and committing, then we sleep together and we're not compatible sexually?"

"I'm glad you brought that up. Another myth is that sexual compatibility is some kind of Holy Grail that makes a relationship work. We think we need to sleep together as an experiment in compatibility. But *chemistry* is the real determinant, and you can discover that without having sex, provided you date long enough to get past the enchantment stage. Almost any new relationship feels exciting, so you need time to see if it's lasting chemistry.

"When you have chemistry with someone, you can't stop touching and kissing, looking into each other's eyes. You banter and flirt and tease. None of that requires sex. Get it?"

"I got it!"

"Chemistry is the real determinant of sexual compatibility and you can discover that without having sex."

"Frankly, the rest is just plumbing and hormones! You can teach each other and learn about the mechanics of sex in the context of your commitment, in the context of marriage. All you need is an open mind and a couple of good books on sex.

"You find out how open-minded a guy

is by talking about sex once you've made a commitment. You discuss one another's attitudes, experiences, and fantasies to determine basic compatibility. Does that make sense?"

Kelly considered her past relationships. "This is truly eye-opening. I've never experienced it, but I'm starting to see how powerful it might be to wait." She frowned, as another thought occurred to her.

"There's just one more thing. I'm a very passionate person. When I'm really attracted to a guy, it's hard for me to not touch him, kiss him, and that gets me…"

"Horny?" Martha asked with a smile.

Kelly squirmed. "Uh, yep, that's it. I can get really stirred up. How do I handle that?"

"You have to avoid situations in which those feelings can be easily acted on. That's why you don't go to his house or invite him to yours for a long time, not until you're certain that you're ready to become lovers or that you can refrain. You decide about sex together, in advance, *never* in the heat of the moment.

"It's very difficult to overcome sexual arousal once it reaches a certain level. That's why it's vital to plan ahead and put structures in place to protect yourself.

"While you're dating, you need to learn to control your *behavior* instead of acting however you feel. This helps you develop good habits for your life together.

Emotions and Love

"Imagine you're married and you're having a bad day. You're irritable. Then he does something like forgetting to run an important errand. You're ticked off. If you speak from your emotions, what do you say to him, in what tone of voice?"

"It's not a pretty picture," Kelly said.

"And what's the impact on your husband, on your marriage?"

"Not good."

"Now imagine that you *justify* saying something nasty to your mate because *that's how you feel.* What if he follows suit? Not very functional, is it?"

"No, it's not. I've been around couples who do that and it's awful. I don't want a marriage like that."

"Right, Kelly. There are different kinds of feelings, some very important to acknowledge and others not. For example, if you're out on a date with a guy and you feel unsafe, I hope that you pay attention to that and get out of there."

"Yes, I get that one. I have pretty good radar for men who are strange or unsafe. I've met a couple of them at singles events and I can almost feel the hair on the back of my neck go up."

"Good. But there are also 'whims of emotion' that you don't want to indulge."

Kelly thought about that. "Like infatuation."

"Right, but keep going."

"Well, there's anger, and um, sexual arousal."

She thought harder. "Then there's fear. Sometimes I'm afraid that if I don't do or say the right thing, the guy I'm falling for will go away. But then I just end up latching onto a guy instead of letting things unfold naturally."

"Exactly. It's not healthy to follow every whim of emotion. Instead, you should cultivate *sustainable* feelings that act as a barometer for your life. What might those be?"

"This is harder." Kelly frowned, thinking. "One thing that comes to mind is having an overall positive attitude about life. If I'm unhappy every day for weeks or months I might question if I'm on the right path in my life."

"Good—that's right. Keep going."

"Well, when I picture myself with the right guy, I feel happy and content."

> *"The goal is sustainable feelings of well being - joy and gratitude each day, an overall optimism about life that you cultivate through focusing on the positive."*

"Right, though even the happiest of couples go through rough patches. Here's the upshot about emotions, dating, and marriage:

"The goal is *sustainable* feelings of well being—joy and gratitude each day, an overall optimism about life that you cultivate through focusing on the positive. In relationships, it's the emotional safety of knowing that someone is trustworthy and that you want the same things and are emotionally available to one another. Together, you feel joy in sharing the day, your hopes and dreams, and the pursuit of them. It's the joy of giving for the sake of giving, not to garner something in return. Does this make sense?"

"That sounds wonderful," Kelly said softly.

"These kinds of feelings and emotions run in the background, like the operating system on your computer. When you're stressed, they may recede, but later the overall good feelings come back.

"Whims of emotion are guided by immediate life events. You get stuck in traffic and feel irritated. Someone says something nasty to you and it hurts. You get the flu and wallow in self-pity. You make out with a guy and get horny.

"The goal is to have balanced emotions in yourself and to choose someone equally well-balanced and healthy.

"Your partner isn't there to make your life complete; rather, you share the bounty of your lives with one another."

Check Your Barometers: Values and Behavior

Martha stopped, let Kelly take more notes, and then asked, "How does all of this resonate with you?"

Kelly finished writing and looked up thoughtfully. "It sounds powerful and healthy." She paused. "But what do I act on, if not my feelings?"

"Think about it—I'm sure you know the answer."

Kelly sighed again. "It all comes back to values, doesn't it? I feel so embarrassed that I never put this together before now. I always thought of myself as a person with good values, but I can see that I haven't been true to them when it comes to men."

"That's a powerful admission, and one that will help you move forward. Values are the ultimate barometer for life success. Feelings come and go, and are definitely NOT the best guide! Values influence how you treat another person and how you expect to be treated in return.

"*Behavior* indicates values—you see it in yourself and in others.

> *Tip: "Align your behavior with your values, not with your feelings."*

If you value creating a healthy relationship with a strong foundation, you take your time to get to know someone. You let your *values* run the show, not your fear that he might get frustrated with your pace and leave.

"Align your behavior with your values, not your feelings. Look for the same in him."

Martha encouraged her to put a stake in the ground about her sexuality with men. Though it seemed impossible to fulfill, Kelly agreed to put off sex a minimum of six months. She wasn't yet sold on the idea of waiting until marriage.

"Now I want you to keep all of this in mind for this exercise." With Martha's guidance, Kelly leaned back, closed her eyes, breathed deeply, and envisioned her future with her soul mate and husband. She thought to herself…

I am with my soul mate, my beloved husband for life. We enjoy a loving connection: intellectually, emotionally, spiritually, and sexually. Every day, we thank God for having found one another. We laugh easily together, play together in many ways. We support each other in achieving our dreams regarding work, life, and spirit.

He is a loving man, devoted to me, always putting our relationship above other life demands. He is inspired by me, telling others in our life how lucky he is to have me. My love for him grows each day. We respect and cherish one another. He shares my values and acts with integrity.

We easily and lovingly resolve conflicts. When feelings are hurt, we care. We get out the emotional bandages and fix it together. Our understanding is to always protect the precious relationship that we share. We nurture our romantic connection.

I see us walking together on a beautiful beach, hand in hand. We smile at each other as we pick up sea shells and comment on the spectacular sunset. It is one vacation trip in a lifetime of simple pleasures. We couldn't be happier.

Kelly wrote her "vision statement" in the present tense, as if it were already true. Her homework was to type it in a nice font, print it, post it prominently, and read it every morning and evening. "This way," Martha told her, "you make your vision a part of you, a part of your very inner workings, so that anything that doesn't match it holds no appeal for you. By focusing on your vision, and infusing it with positive emotions as you do so, you attract exactly that. There's no room for anything else, and when you meet someone who doesn't match your vision, you naturally veer away and continue your search."

Tip: "Create a vision statement and make it a part of you, a part of your very inner workings, so that anything that doesn't match it loses its appeal to you."

Armed with her new process, her vision statement, and her commitment to self-care, Kelly braced herself to tackle dating. She was determined to do things right this time.

The Eighth Temptation:

Rushing into Relationships

Chapter Eight

Kelly re-activated her online dating accounts. The first guy she had coffee with, Mike, was fifteen minutes late and walked in wearing fashionably faded jeans, tennis shoes, and a tee shirt. Though cute, he seemed a little too aware of his charms.

Kelly's radar told her that Mike expected her to deliver all the goodies and ask little of him. She decided to test her assumptions. When he asked for another date, she told him to call later after she checked her calendar. She gave him her work number and special web-based email address, one that she could easily change if she had problems with a guy she met online.

The next day, Mike sent a rambling email, ending with:

> *If you'd like to get together again, call me.*
> *Mike*

Kelly wrote back:

> *I have a policy of not calling guys or accepting an email request for a date. Here's my work number in case you lost it.*
> *Kelly.*

Mike called. Instead of asking for a date, he rambled on about himself, bragging about his business success and all the local celebrities he knew. Eventually, he suggested she come over Friday night and catch a good flick on his new fifty-two inch flat-screen H.D. TV. Kelly suggested a lunch date for the following week. Mike argued, insisting on dinner at his place another night. It felt like a power struggle and Kelly decided to pull the plug.

"What you get in the beginning with a guy is the best you'll get. If what he offers up front doesn't make you feel special, pass."

"You know what Mike, I'm sorry but this isn't going to work. I appreciate that you took time to meet me and call me, but this simply isn't a match for me."

"How do you know this isn't right? You don't even know me." Mike sounded irritated.

"I realize it doesn't make sense to you, but it does to me." She carefully chose neutral terms like "it's not a match" instead of "*you're* not right for me," keeping her voice calm. She ended the call quickly, wishing him well, and clicked off.

Kelly was proud of herself. She'd listened to her gut and acted when it didn't feel right. She remembered Martha's warning: "What you get in the beginning with a guy is the best you'll get. If what he offers up front doesn't feel wonderful, pass."

She also felt proud that she hadn't played games. She didn't pretend interest, accept a date she didn't want, and dump him later. ["That's one of the worst things women do," Martha had told her. "Because we're so uncomfortable saying no, we say yes when we don't mean it. At the last minute, we cancel with a lame excuse or, worse yet, he spends the evening with a limp noodle who can't wait to escape him."]

Tip: "Don't accept a date you don't want. Saying yes when you don't mean it makes for a miserable evening for two people."

She even thanked him as she declined. ["Guys are used to being cut off when women aren't interested. Remember, it takes guts for a guy to pursue a woman. He takes a lot of rejection along the way, so express your appreciation for his willingness to take the risk."]

Though Kelly itched to tell Mike what a jerk he was, she heeded Martha's coaching: "Don't create drama. It diminishes your pride. Be calm and neutral and break the connection in a gentle way, unless you sense that a guy might be dangerous. That demands a much more forceful stance."

No Chemistry: Too Much Rationalizing

The next guy Kelly met, Gary, showed up on time, nicely dressed. Gary did all the right things. He jumped up to get Kelly's coffee, threw away the old napkins when they were done, pulled out her chair when she came back from the restroom, and listened attentively to everything she said. He seemed modest about his achievements, though he was the CFO of a multi-million dollar company.

> "When you say no, express appreciation for the invitation. Guys take a lot of risk and get a lot of rejection along the way, and rarely do women appreciate what that takes."

But Kelly felt absolutely no chemistry. In every other way, he was perfect. Torn, she accepted another date.

A few days later, over brunch on Sunday, Kelly experienced the same conflict. Gary was intelligent, had a good sense of humor, and evidenced a well-rounded life with many common interests. Unfortunately, no sparks flew on that date, either. That night, she expressed her frustration to Martha.

> Tip: "Don't create drama; it diminishes your pride. Instead, be calm and neutral, and break off connections gently."

"I thought if I didn't feel sparks right away, I might with time."

"Has that ever worked, Kelly?"

"A couple of times I didn't feel wildly attracted right away and the guy kind of grew on me."

"And what happened after that?"

Kelly thought about it. "In the long run, I guess I didn't really feel the desire to make it work. When problems came up, I bailed."

"Those are examples of 'settle for' relationships, meaning that you know deep down this person isn't a soul mate, but he's good enough for now."

"But Gary is perfect in so many ways! How could I *not* be attracted to him? Maybe if I…"

"Maybe, but first, let's give it the kiss test. Picture yourself sitting across from Gary. Now, can you imagine your lips on his?"

"No way! He's a great guy, but if he tried to kiss me I wouldn't like it. I might put up with it, but I wouldn't enjoy it. I can't explain it, Martha, but I have no interest in touching him."

"That's the bottom line then."

"This is so disappointing," Kelly sighed. "Though I don't know Gary that well, my gut tells me he's got a great heart and exceptional character. I feel so emotionally safe with him. Why can't this work?"

"Basic chemistry is an important part of the match. Can you imagine your sex life in a marriage with a guy whose touch repels you?"

Kelly got the picture. "You're right. I'm a very passionate person. I can't imagine being married to someone without wanting to share physical intimacy."

"And don't forget that it's no bargain for him. Imagine what it would do to him to know that his wife didn't welcome his touch."

"I've always been wildly attracted to the wrong guys. What if I'm not capable of attraction to a nice guy?" Kelly felt terribly discouraged.

"Trust me: time, patience, and adherence to the process will bring everything into focus. There are many, many good guys out there, and at least one you'll find completely attractive. The process that you're practicing helps re-adjust your feelings so that good guys become attractive to you.

"Focus on the big picture of your life, your vision. The cost of choosing a partner just because you're eager to marry is very high."

They spent a few more minutes discussing the situation and what to do. After saying goodnight to Martha, Kelly called Gary and gently told him that it wasn't a love connection. She offered friendship but acknowledged that he might not be comfortable with that.

Though clearly disappointed, Gary didn't push her. In fact, he thanked her for being so honest. "Most women don't take the time to explain why they don't want to go out anymore. It's refreshing to have someone do it so graciously."

Kelly hung up the phone feeling warmly toward Gary. It felt good to handle relationship issues in a straightforward way. Oddly, she felt a sense of regret, a lost opportunity. But Martha had warned her about that as well.

"When people communicate openly and honestly, Kelly, it promotes emotional intimacy. As you practice that with guys who are capable of the same, you may experience feelings of attraction. Paradoxically, those feelings may surge at strange times like when you end a relationship. That's a good thing because it gives you a barometer of what it's like to have a positive connection with a good guy. But don't mistake that for evidence that he's 'the one.'

> *"When people communicate openly and honestly, it promotes emotional intimacy. It is natural to experience feelings of attraction as you practice that with guys who are capable of the same, but don't mistake that for evidence that he's 'the one.'"*

"It's normal to feel attracted to a wide variety of people, but the right guy is a cut above in every way that's meaningful to *you*. Meanwhile, enjoy those feelings with different men but don't feel compelled to act on them."

"What if my feelings for Gary change, Martha? What if I'm so confused I can't see straight, and later on I feel totally different? He might be taken by then!"

"That's a possibility. Sometimes a woman initially feels no chemistry with a guy, meets him again months or years later, or in a different context, and then it's completely different. You might run into Gary in six months and suddenly he'll be everything you want, chemistry and all. But *until that day*, trust how you feel *right now* and go with that. That's vital for developing your inner compass."

After Gary, Kelly had a couple of coffee and lunch dates with guys who weren't even close to a match. She politely declined future dates, thanking them for taking the time to meet. It felt good to not waste time with guys she wasn't interested in. Then the tide turned in an unexpected direction.

✳ ✳ ✳

At dinner with one of her best girlfriends, Jamie, Kelly spotted a really cute guy at another table.

"Is that guy staring at us?" she whispered.

"No, he's staring at *you*! What a fox!" Jamie whispered back, grinning.

"No, I don't think so. Really? Do you think he's looking at me?" Kelly felt like a high school girl with butterflies in her stomach. She refused to stare back, shifting her focus back to Jamie. Ten minutes later, she looked up to see "the fox" standing at her table, smiling at her. He was even cuter up close, with wavy brown hair and blue eyes.

"Excuse me," he said. "I couldn't help but notice you from across the room. This is a little strange, and I don't normally do this, but I'm curious to know if you're single..."

"Yes, I am," Kelly answered, feeling herself blush.

"In that case, my name's Chris. Is it okay if I call to ask you out?"

Kelly almost blurted "yes!" But somehow, she restrained herself. She took her time, answering slowly, "I don't feel comfortable giving my number to strangers."

Jamie almost choked on her sip of wine. She grabbed her napkin and coughed into it, her eyes widening.

Kelly waited, feeling tense.

"Sure! Of course," Chris sputtered. "Uh, how about if I give you my number, or my email address, and if you feel comfortable, you can call me, and then I'll ask you out?"

"Well, okay," Kelly answered demurely, again refraining from the over-the-top enthusiasm she'd demonstrated in the past.

Chris took out a business card and wrote a personal email address and home phone number on the back, giving it to Kelly. He smiled warmly and told her he'd really love to hear from her.

After he left, Jamie blurted out, "Are you crazy? You almost let him get away!"

Kelly smiled. "I know," she said.

"What's gotten into you?"

"I'm just making some changes in the way I go about dating and one of them is to be more laid back. I'm so done with making it easy for guys to pick me up."

Jamie looked at her like she was a different person and Kelly sensed her friend's growing respect.

* * *

Kelly did nothing with Chris' information for two days. Then she sent a short email:

> *Hi Chris,*
> *Remember me? We met at La Duni a few nights ago. I would enjoy hearing from you at my office. The number is...*
> *Kelly*

She refrained from including tons of encouragement in the mistaken belief that guys needed it in order to take the next step. Martha called it *building emotional muscle.*

Chris called almost immediately and they chatted for a few minutes. He asked for a dinner date and Kelly suggested lunch instead. She insisted on meeting there and planning no more than an hour or so.

Kelly recalled Martha's warning her about marathon dates with guys she didn't know. "You have lots of time later for long, romantic dates, Kelly. The first three dates are basically for discovery of whether or not there's any point in dating. It takes time and conversation to discover whether or not he's an emotionally available person who shares your values and wants what you want. Long dinner dates with wine and candlelight contribute to emotional and sexual attachment, so avoid those for the first few weeks."

> *Tip: "Use the first three dates to determine whether or not there's any point in dating."*

* * *

Kelly prepared for her lunch date with Chris by reviewing her notes from the last session with Martha, jotting down a few bullet points on a card and putting it in her bag. It felt more like going for a job interview than a date. *This guy doesn't know it,* she thought with a little smile, *but he's interviewing today for the job of boyfriend-leading-to-husband!*

Per Martha's coaching and now her regular practice on first dates with strangers, Kelly arrived twenty minutes early, parking away from the restaurant entrance. "You can't be too safe. Don't let him see your car until you get to know him, for two reasons: (1) He can find your home address with a license plate number and (2) He can make assumptions about you based on your car. Get to know the person and let him get to know you before you reveal your lifestyle."

She sat at a table, reading a book, waiting for noon to roll around. At two minutes before twelve, Chris walked in and looked around. *Score one for him*, she thought. *He's early: a good sign.*

Chris greeted her with a warm smile. They ordered lunch and chatted about what they did for work, where they grew up, number of siblings, where they went to school, and so on. Chris was easy to talk to. He listened well and seemed to understand her. There was definitely chemistry between them. She felt her cheeks growing rosy as he gazed at her with obvious admiration.

Kelly excused herself for the powder room where she quickly reviewed her notes. Here comes the tough part, she thought.

Back at the table, Kelly started the real conversation. "So, Chris, how long have you been single?"

Kelly's notes for first dates:

- Meet at the venue (no picking you up at your home until you know him and check his references); keep the date short—30 minutes to one hour; no alcohol

- Keep the main goal in mind: to determine if it's worthwhile to have a second date; what to look for:

- A touch of chemistry

- Good manners, thoughtfulness, positive attitude

- Stories from his life that indicate good values

He laughed. "I've never been married, if that's what you mean. How about you?"

"Me neither," Kelly said. "How long has it been since your last relationship?"

Chris looked a bit uncomfortable. "Uh, it's been a few weeks." He stopped.

"How many weeks?" Kelly persisted.

"Well, about four, actually. But we were headed that way for a long time," he added hastily.

"How long were you together?" Kelly asked, staying cool.

"A couple of years." Chris looked even more uncomfortable.

"What happened—why did you break up?" Kelly asked.

"You know, Kelly, most women don't ask these kinds of questions on the first date," Chris said, a bit defensively.

"I realize that, but let me ask you something. Are you attracted to me?" Kelly could hardly believe she'd had the guts to ask, but it felt good to put it on the table.

"Of course! You're gorgeous!"

"Okay. Well, I feel the same way about you, so I guess it's fair to say that we're headed for another date, right?"

"I hope so."

Kelly took a breath. "So, if that goes well and we have another, that means potentially getting close. I don't want to go there without knowing a few things, and I don't mean just vital statistics."

"It's only a first date."

"You're right, and I take it in that spirit. We're just beginning to get to know each other."

He looked relieved. "Okay, understood."

More relaxed now, he briefly shared the story of his two and a half year relationship with Sherry, his ex-fiancée. He made it sound like they discovered they were incompatible and broke it off.

Kelly didn't press for more. She felt proud of herself that she'd found out about his latest relationship on the first date. After that, they talked about things they had in common, books they'd recently read. She discovered that he had a big, close family—two brothers, loving parents, aunts, uncles, and cousins all very connected. Things clicked between them, and time flew.

Kelly looked at her watch in surprise. "It's way past time for me to get back to work." She gathered her bag and stood.

"Wait," Chris asked. "I'd like to set up another date. Would you have dinner with me tomorrow night?"

Instead of jumping to "yes!," Kelly paused, took a breath, and forced herself to remember the next steps.

"Let's take it a little slower than that. How about lunch next week?"

Chris looked surprised but agreed. They scheduled something for the following Wednesday. As they walked to the door, Kelly stopped and made the excuse of visiting the powder room again, saying good bye with a little hand shake. Chris held her hand for a moment, gazing warmly into her eyes, and her skin tingled.

She watched him leave, and then went to the restroom for five minutes, per Martha's coaching. "Don't walk to the car until you know him and check his references. You can't be too safe."

Kelly knew where Chris worked. She called his office pretending to need information for business reasons. She did an internet background search. So far, he checked out.

Last, Kelly followed Martha's coaching and quietly reflected on her brief time with Chris. Her gut told her that he was basically a good guy. But she knew she didn't yet know enough to open up.

Still, she felt a small surge of excitement. Over the next few days, she thought about Chris from time to time, looking forward to their next date.

Kelly and Chris hit it off at lunch the following week. They talked non-stop and time slipped away: two hours. Chris asked for a dinner date and Kelly agreed to Sunday night the following weekend. She insisted they meet at the restaurant. Dinner went exceptionally well, and Kelly thought maybe she'd found 'the one.' Chris seemed to share the same values and want the same things. The sparks flew between them. What could possibly be wrong with this picture? Kelly and Chris went out for two more dinner dates, and then it was time for her weekend with Martha.

* * *

Kelly couldn't wait to tell her about Chris. She launched in, beaming. "His name is Chris and so far, he a real match! He's sweet, charming, sexy, smart, successful, and so much fun! He's falling for me too, I can feel it. Martha, he's wonderful!"

Martha remained neutral. "That sounds great, Kelly, but let's take a step back. You really can't possibly know someone after just a couple of weeks."

"I know. It has been only a couple of weeks. But he really is wonderful."

"If you decide after three or four dates that the guy you're seeing is 'the one', you emotionally invest in that reality. At that point, how open are you to seeing anything that contradicts what you believe?"

"I guess not very open."

"Right. This is the problem with deciding early in a relationship that someone is 'the one': it makes you very selective about what you see, filtering out any experiences that might undermine your assumption. You have a history of choosing badly when it comes to men so snap judgments are very risky for you. True?"

"Yes. But how can I avoid doing that?"

"The first step is to practice saying 'we'll see—I don't know yet if he's the one' when a relationship is new. Try it now—use the actual words."

> "Deciding early in a relationship that someone is 'the one' makes you very selective about what you see. You tend to filter out any experiences that might undermine your assumption because you've invested too much too soon."

"We'll See": The Right Attitude for Pacing

"*We'll see about Chris.* I don't know if he's 'the one,' and I'm okay with that." She paused, letting herself absorb the impact of the words.

"Wow, it feels really liberating to say that. I don't feel like I have to prove anything."

"Great! Try to maintain that stance for the foreseeable future. Now, tell me all about him."

"He takes me out to nice places, doesn't try too hard to be intimate, and respects my boundaries. We've kissed good night, but when I stop there, he's respectful, a real gentleman. We have tons in common."

Martha smiled. "What's his track record with women?"

She revealed Chris' engagement to Sherry, but didn't know anything prior to that relationship. Martha asked more questions about Chris and Sherry, but Kelly came up with blanks.

"Do you see where I'm going with this?" Martha asked.

"You're trying to look deeper at Chris' personal history. I'm embarrassed to say that I don't know that much. We enjoy being together so much, we have so much to talk about that's fun, and I don't want to mess up the mood by bringing up the past again."

"Mess up the mood?" Martha asked softly.

Kelly sighed. "Here I go again. As usual, I'm focusing on making everything perfectly romantic from the get-go! Will I ever get this?"

Temptation: Rushing Into Relationships

"Sounds like you're confronting the **Eighth Temptation**, Kelly: *rushing into relationships* instead of pacing like we've discussed. The problem is that it blinds you to the reality in front of you because you invest too much too soon. Here's the test: Are you willing to say goodbye to Chris if he turns out to have a deal-breaking situation in his life?"

Kelly felt miserable. "I don't like thinking about it, but yes, I'd rather find out now than down the road."

"I'm glad to hear that. It's important that you're willing to let go of a guy at any stage of a developing relationship. Most women, once they meet a guy who could be 'the one,' grab on desperately with both hands, as if he's the last ship that will ever sail into port. Good marriage decisions are not made that way. You have too much at stake to succumb to the temptation of rushing into something that may be all wrong for you.

"*We'll see* is appropriate for at least the first six months in a new relationship, and maybe longer. Can you get on board with that?"

Kelly agreed that she would. Martha helped her outline the conversation for her date with Chris that night. Kelly's bubble had definitely burst, but she was determined to stay on her new path, even if it meant saying good-bye to Chris.

* * *

Kelly let the conversation go the way it usually did on her dates with Chris. They chatted about work, their week, and some of their common interests. She knew she had to shift the conversation so she took a powder room break to interrupt the flow and double-check her notes.

Kelly's notes:

- Use open-ended questions to ask about his relationship with Sherry

- Make it safe for him to open up and don't stop until you have the full picture of what happened and where he is today emotionally

- Drill down: when you hear something that sounds important to him, ask more questions about it

---

When she returned, she shifted to a much more serious tone. "Chris," she began, "I've been thinking and I realize I still don't know a lot about your past relationships.

"I'm concerned about being the transitional woman in your life. Wait," she said as Chris started to speak, "please don't try to reassure me just yet. I have a few questions if you don't mind."

He assured her that he didn't, so she dove in. "Why exactly did you and Sherry break up, and *how* did it happen?" She sat back, prepared to listen with an open mind.

Chris sighed. "This isn't easy for me to talk about, but if it helps you I will." He shared the story again, this time with more detail. Kelly asked questions from time to time along the way, encouraging Chris to open up more, zeroing in on things that seemed important.

Chris and Sherry had met through mutual friends. She had been divorced with a five year old son, an emotionally needy little boy who had been traumatized by his Dad's departure from his life. Sherry, though financially stable due to her wealthy ex-husband, had felt a tremendous amount of pressure to fulfill her role as a single Mom. Chris had tried to help out as much as he could. He'd bonded with Sherry's son, who'd seemed to need a father figure, as his real father rarely saw him.

Chris seemed uncomfortable talking about his engagement to Sherry, but Kelly pressed him for the details. He'd proposed after a year and a half of dating, and yes, he'd given Sherry a gorgeous diamond ring. Yes, he'd been in love with her [though he tried to use the expression "I *thought* I was in love"]. Kelly stated frankly that she didn't respect the idea that you "think you're in love," you either are or you are not, and why propose to someone you don't love?

Martha insisted these were critical questions to ask men: were you in love? Have you ever been in love? "You don't want a guy who's never been in love, or who has but can't acknowledge it. Love is the essence of a relationship, and if he doesn't get that by now, you're in trouble."

Martha also drilled it into Kelly's head that questioning a guy's feelings and behavior with the last woman was the quickest way to find out (a) how emotionally available he is, and (b) how he will treat you. "If he's still angry, sad, or in love, he's not ready to devote himself to you. If he blames her for all of the problems, or he says he just fell out of love, or they grew apart, then he's not taking responsibility for his part in the relationship or he's not telling you the real story. Either way, you're not getting a good deal."

Kelly asked who initiated the breakup, and Chris acknowledged that Sherry had. "Why?" Kelly wanted to know. Chris hesitated.

"Chris, pretend we're not on a date. We're just two people talking about our lives and getting to know each other."

Something seemed to shift in Chris, as if he finally gave up whatever he'd been trying to protect. He opened up, no longer hesitating to bare all.

Sherry had broken up with him because she hadn't been able to stand the pressure. Chris had become increasingly resentful of her lack of availability to spend alone time with him. She'd been reluctant to hire babysitters, so they'd stayed home most of the time where her focus had been on her little boy. That had left very little for Chris and he'd found it difficult. Everything had come to a head one night in a huge argument that had ended with Sherry giving back the ring and stating that she couldn't give him what he needed.

"It's for the best," Chris ended, looking absolutely miserable. Kelly reflected carefully, considering her options.

"Chris, you still love Sherry, don't you?" she asked softly.

"Kelly, this is not at all what I planned for tonight," Chris said, but she stopped him.

"I know. But life has a funny way of rearranging our plans, doesn't it? You don't even have to answer, Chris. It's written all over your face—of course you still love Sherry. It's only been a few weeks and you were together a long time."

Kelly thought quickly. "If you really love her, and there's no deal-breaker, then you owe it to yourself to work it out if you can. Are there any deal-breakers: drugs or alcohol?"

"No! There's absolutely nothing wrong with Sherry."

"Okay. So here's the deal. Even though I'm not a Mom yet myself, I know it's a hard job, and a very important one. If you love her, you have to accept that her son is her top priority. Show her you care by pitching in, not by making demands. You can work out ways to have your separate time together when he's sleeping, or you can get babysitters at times, but when he's with her, her attention is supposed to be on her child. After all, he's a little boy who's lost his Dad. Can you handle that?"

Chris looked like a weight lifted from his shoulders. They talked about how he could be more supportive of Sherry, with Kelly giving him tips from a woman's perspective.

When they parted, Chris thanked her for being so understanding. "I'm kind of sorry it didn't work out for us, Kelly. You're an incredible woman. Some guy is going to be extremely lucky when he finds you."

Kelly drove home in a daze. This was definitely not the outcome she'd envisioned for the evening! Paradoxically, she felt empowered, strengthened somehow.

She thought about Martha's coaching: "If his heart is with someone else, he can't give you the devotion that you want and deserve. Can he fall in love with you? Yes, to a degree. But until a guy's heart is really free of the last woman he deeply loved, you will be the transitional woman."

Kelly realized that by asking the right questions, and making it safe for Chris to open up, she'd uncovered the truth. The fact was that he wasn't even close to being over Sherry! What had happened tonight—going their separate ways, he back to Sherry and she back to the dating game—was exactly what was going to happen in the long run. She'd succeeded in sparing herself the heartache of getting attached and feeling hopeful about an emotionally unavailable guy.

She was learning, really growing! This process was opening her eyes in ways she couldn't have imagined. She smiled to herself. *Look out, world, I'm ready for anything!*

The Ninth Temptation:

Taking the Lead

Chapter Nine

Kelly was armed and dangerous. She knew how to set up her dates and she knew what to ask. She knew what to avoid and what to look for. She had a process and tools that worked. Her single girlfriends marveled and scratched their heads, trying to figure out what Kelly was up to. She smiled coyly and insisted she was simply learning to date smarter.

Kelly practiced on lots of guys. Though she wanted and intended to meet the right guy, the timing wasn't yet right. Meanwhile, she learned from each experience with each new guy.

Kelly thought she was just about through with the temptations. "I'm ready for Mr. Right!" she declared. "I think I've had enough practice." Martha smiled and reminded Kelly that the timing was in God's hands. No one could predict when, where, or how the right person showed up.

The next few candidates were total duds. She went out with guys with no career directions, guys who were physically unattractive to her, and narcissistic guys with no ability to love and cherish a woman. Her radar served her well, saving her tons of time and energy.

The short first dates really worked: Kelly no longer endured endlessly long, boring dinner dates with men in whom she had no interest. Now, if a guy was all wrong for her, she wasted no more than thirty minutes at a coffee shop.

Martha encouraged Kelly to hang in there. "Just because you meet a few frogs doesn't mean you should give up on the Prince!" she laughed. Just as Kelly's discouragement reached an all-time high, her luck turned for the better.

Kelly met Josh through an online dating service. She was instantly mesmerized by his bedroom eyes, his movie star looks, and his radio

DJ voice. He was hot—no doubt about it! She practically had to take a cold shower after their first date. Chemistry? No problem! Values? Well, she'd have to check that out further. Even though a little voice inside whispered that Josh was a long shot [how many really hot guys turned out to be good husband material?], she set up a second date.

Over lunch, Kelly and Josh discovered they had a lot in common. Kelly breathed a secret sigh of relief after grilling him about his past relationships and not finding any red flags. Josh was more conservative than his looks implied. Had he dated? Yes, but he didn't seem to be a player. Yes, he'd been in love and she'd left him to go back to an ex. Yes, he wanted to find the right woman; he wanted marriage and a family.

This is too good to be true! Kelly thought as she drove home later. She was attracted to Josh, not just physically, but intellectually as well. It turned out he was an avid photographer and loved historical novels. He had a master's degree in communications and worked as an advertising executive. He was funny, too, making her laugh with stories about the eccentric people he often met in the business. She could hardly wait for the next date.

A week later, Josh finally called, claiming work overload. They talked for thirty minutes before he asked her out again. He suggested dinner Friday night, four days away. That was a good sign, as Kelly no longer accepted last minute dates. "Planning ahead is a sign of the ability to make a commitment," Martha told her. "It's not enough evidence to know for sure, but it's an important piece of the picture.

"Early on, you should never accept a date less than three days in advance. That helps you weed out the guys who have no persistence or ability to plan ahead. You don't want to be the girl he calls after his other date falls through. If he wants to go out with you, he'll ask for another time on your calendar. Don't be afraid to say no a couple of times to a guy you really like. If he's really into you, he won't be put off."

Josh and Kelly's Friday night date couldn't have been better. Kelly was enchanted. They laughed and talked non-

Tip: "Early on, you should never accept a date less than three days in advance: planning ahead is a sign of the ability to make a commitment."

stop. The sparks were mutual, she was certain. At one point Josh took Kelly's hand and held it, stroking her fingers. She thought she was going to pass out she was so excited. *Whoa!* She told herself sternly. *Get a grip!* She hoped he would ask for another date but all he did was hug her, telling her he'd had a great time. "You're adorable, Kelly," Josh said, gazing into her eyes. He leaned in and kissed her. Her heart leaped. Kelly went home certain that he was wild about her.

Temptation: Taking the Lead

Ten days went by with no call from Josh. Kelly's anxiety shot up. She called Martha, wanting to know why she couldn't call or email Josh, remind him she was there. "What if he lost my number? What if he got really busy with work, time slipped away, and now he's embarrassed because he didn't follow through before now? What's wrong with giving a guy some encouragement, you know, let him know I'm still interested?"

"So you're saying you don't think he's smart enough to find your phone number again if he lost it."

"No! I'm not saying that, I just..."

"Furthermore, you're saying that he's not perceptive enough to figure out that you want him to call again."

"I uh..."

"Let me ask you something, Kelly. What do you think Josh does when he goes after a new client? Do you think he waits for the client to call and reassure him before he asks for the next meeting?"

"No, of course not."

"Of course not. So, tell me what's really going on."

"I guess I'm just impatient. Besides, this is the twenty first century! Women can ask men out—we don't have to sit waiting for them to do all the calling."

"Have you ever asked a guy out early in the relationship or after he dropped the ball? How did it go?"

Kelly remembered a couple of guys that she'd asked out early on. "Not good. One guy I asked out for our third date. By our fifth date, we were hanging out at my place, and after that, he never asked me out again! I ended it before it went any further. Now that I think about it, I can't ever remember having a good feeling after asking a guy out. Something changed and left me feeling frustrated."

"Perhaps you couldn't discern how much interest he had in you. Could that be it?"

"Yes! That's it. I couldn't tell how much he wanted the relationship. I thought I was a modern woman in charge but instead I felt powerless."

"You just put your finger on the paradox, Kelly. For some things, taking charge makes us feel powerful, while for other things, taking charge leaves us feeling less in control. For women, dating is one of those. Which brings us to the **Ninth Temptation:** *taking the lead* instead of taking your cues. We lose our power as women when we take the lead in a relationship. After years of stumbling around on this one in my own life, I finally realized that I needed to let go, let the guy lead, and then decide if I liked where it was going. That gave me my power back. It allowed me to see what *his intentions* were, to feel my feminine power. Sounds ancient, doesn't it?"

> *"We lose our power as women when we take the lead in a relationship. Let go, let the guy lead, and decide if you like where it's going. Letting him lead will show you what his intentions are and keep your feminine power intact."*

"In a way, but I have another question. Josh acted so romantic and affectionate. Why was he all over me and then didn't bother to call?!"

"Just because he's momentarily enchanted with you *doesn't mean he's intentional in pursuing you for a relationship.* Men are notorious for being romantic one minute and incommunicado the next. If you're willing to wait, you'll find out what's really going on. Can you go along with that for now?"

"I'm not sure I quite get it, but for the time being, I'll let Josh take the lead if he wants to." When they wrapped up, Martha promised a surprise that weekend.

The Dance of Love: Taking Your Cues

Saturday morning, Kelly pulled up at the address Martha gave her. In dismay, she read the sign over the door, wondering if she'd gotten the information wrong. "Ballroom Dance" it said, followed by: Swing, Latin, and Waltz.

Inside, Martha stood chatting with a guy she introduced as Marc, who flashed a huge smile at Kelly as he turned to greet her. "I've heard so much about you!" Dressed in a black tee shirt and black jeans with dark hair and a lean, athletic frame, he looked exactly the way Kelly imagined a dancer should look. *Why does Martha want me here?* she wondered as she shook his hand.

"Kelly, I've scheduled up some dance lessons for you today, for a dual purpose. Relax," she said, as Kelly's eyes widened, "Be open to the experience.

"Marc will take over from here, then you and I will talk later. Have fun!" Kelly's mouth fell open as Martha exited, waving good-bye. Marc gave Kelly a special pair of dance shoes to put on, then took her hand and led her to the dance floor.

The next two hours amazed Kelly; at times, she felt extremely frustrated; at other times, exhilarated. Sweating and exhausted, she changed back into her shoes, and suddenly noticed Martha sitting nearby. Apparently she'd been there for a while, observing.

Marc greeted Martha, who after a bit of conversation asked, "So Marc, how is Katrina? The studio seems to be running like a well-oiled machine."

He laughed. "Yes, she's quite the drill sergeant," he said, glancing at the stunning blond on the other side of the studio who was working with a male student.

"I remember when the two of you met, when was that? Ten years ago?"

"Twelve, actually, and our little girl is now ten!" Marc beamed.

Martha reminisced with Marc, asking questions about how he and Katrina met and dated. At one point she slipped in the question that Kelly knew was meant for her edification. "So who asked who out first, Marc? Did she?"

Marc shook his head, smiling. "Are you kidding? I asked her out three times before she said yes. My friends thought I was crazy, going after this gorgeous dancer who kept turning me down. But I knew she was the one for me and I wasn't about to give up."

"After she said yes, did she turn around and start pursuing you?" Martha asked teasingly.

"Hardly. She let me chase her around, but once I caught her, it was all worth it. She's the best thing that's ever happened to me."

Kelly felt her heart tug listening to Marc speak about his wife. She couldn't help but wonder what it might be like to have a really great guy love her like that, especially after twelve years of marriage.

Martha thanked Marc for working with Kelly and they left. Later, Martha kicked off the next round of Kelly's lessons. "How was your first ballroom dance experience?" she asked after they ordered lunch, smiling.

"It was amazing! I've never seen myself as a dancer but Marc took me through the basic steps of several of the main ballroom dances, and you know what? I found out that with a little instruction, I can actually do it!" Kelly's eyes shone with joy.

"That's great! Now, tell me what you had to learn in order to be successful with the steps."

"There were two main things. First, he taught me to hold my space, which has to do with the tension in my arms and the way we connect, which led straight into leading and following. Even though it looks like the man is doing all the work in ballroom dance, in reality the woman is doing just as much work following as he is leading."

"Was that easy or challenging?"

"Oh my gosh, it was so challenging! First, I had to learn how to hold my arms with just the right tension. I couldn't be a limp noodle or he had nothing to lead. I couldn't be a brick wall or he had to work too hard. The tension had to be just right, and then he could draw me into his space for the dance.

"Then, I had to learn how to follow. If I tried to anticipate his moves, I stepped on his feet. That was embarrassing! I had to wait for him to move and respond at the right moment. If I invaded his space by anticipating his moves, we crashed into each other."

"What else?" Martha asked.

"Marc taught me to be grounded and hold my center. If I started tip-toeing, I got off balance. It's funny, because it looks like the women are tipping over with those high heeled shoes, but in reality they're practically glued to the floor.

"At one point, he did this little exercise. He asked me to hold up my arms with no tension, just kind of limp. Right away, it was obvious that he couldn't do anything with me—the dance didn't happen! Then he asked me to respond to his lead by moving too far forward too fast. That collapsed our space and, again, the dance was over!

"He showed me that it takes strength, grounding, and presence to be a good follower in ballroom. Honestly, Martha, I was exhausted at the end of it! But I have to say it's the most fun I've had in a long time."

"That's wonderful, Kelly! I thought you might enjoy it. So, based on your experience today, what kind of qualities must a man have to be a successful dancer?"

"Clearly, he has to be strong. He has to be comfortable in the role of leader. Aware of where his partner is at all times, taking care to give her the right movements to respond to, taking care not to do anything that hurts her. He has to be *connected*; that's something Marc really emphasized. He can't be in his own little world, not paying attention to his partner because ultimately, ballroom dance isn't about the guy, it's about the woman. A really great male dancer shows off the woman in his arms—makes *her* look great!"

Equal Yet Different

Martha smiled. "You got it. Now, are the roles of men and women *alike* in ballroom dance?"

"No! Not even close. He has his steps, she has hers. The trick is to bring them together and synchronize. That's the beauty of the dance, as Marc explained to me."

> *"In relationships, he has his steps, she has hers. The trick is to bring them together and synchronize. That's the beauty of the dance."*

"Are they equal as partners? I mean in the sense of their contribution to the dance."

"Absolutely! You can't have the dance without both their contributions, each in their own way."

"I know exactly why you gave me this experience, Martha. It's about our roles as men and women. Josh needs to take the lead so I have something to respond to. When he takes a step, I can take the corresponding step. Until he does, my step is an invasion of his space. We both stumble and fall."

"That's it, Kelly, and there's more. If you don't let him take the lead initially, you wind up in a dance where you have to lead all the time. Most women are dissatisfied with that dynamic—again, it may sound like a throwback, but we're hard-wired to enjoy responding to a good man's romantic lead. What was it like for you, with Marc leading?"

"It was wonderful! I felt so feminine, so alive."

"Think about this. If you meet a guy and he fails to take the lead, what does that tell you? Could there be some men who resist leading in relationships? If so, why do you suppose that is?"

Kelly thought about it, frowning. "Maybe the kind of guy who fails to lead is really fearful of rejection, afraid of getting hurt. He's not willing to take emotional risks in order to win the prize."

"And what kind of life partner would a guy like that be?"

"Not a good one! Now that I think about it, that's exactly the way Jason was. He tossed out a few emotional crumbs, and then waited for me to give him the big green light. The next step in the dance was just hanging out, sleeping together. There was never any sense of leadership from him. You know what, Martha? If I had practiced with Jason what I do now, I seriously doubt we would ever have had a first date!" Her eyes lit with understanding.

"What about your strength, Kelly? What did the dance lesson teach you about a woman's strength in a relationship?"

"That I am a strong woman, an equal in every way, yet I can respect the beauty of the dance by letting him lead. This is so liberating!"

✳ ✳ ✳

Two nights later, Josh sent an email:

> *Hi Kelly,*
> *It was really great seeing you the last time we got together. You are such a beautiful woman. If you want to get together again, give me a call.*
> *Josh*

Kelly didn't think twice. She immediately wrote back:

> *Hi Josh,*
> *Good to hear from you. I enjoyed our date as well. I make it my policy not to call guys for dates, so if you want to go out again, here's my number. I realize that might not work for you. In that case, I wish you well.*
> *Kelly*

Ten minutes later, the phone rang.

"Hi Kelly," said Josh. "I just got your email. How are you?"

They chatted a little about not much, and then Josh got to his real purpose.

"I was kind of surprised by your response. Aren't we in the age of equality between men and women? Why is it the guy's responsibility to do all the asking?" He sounded genuinely curious.

"I agree we're equal as men and women, but I find dating works a whole lot better if I let a guy lead at first." She hesitated. "Can I be totally candid with you?"

"Yes, of course."

"Okay. In the past, I jumped in and took over the lead if a guy hesitated even a little bit. But I found that I couldn't tell what his intentions were, and that set me up for disappointment and a lot of wasted time. So, I've learned to take a different approach."

Josh listened quietly. "Okay, Kelly, I hear you, but doesn't a guy deserve to know a woman's intentions? I've also had the experience in the past of wasting my time wining and dining women who have no interest in a relationship. I'm a little gun shy about that myself."

"I understand how you feel, but I'm still not going to jump in there so you don't have to take risks. When you and I went out last time, couldn't you tell how interested I am? Was there anything subtle about the way I kissed you back?"

Josh laughed. "Good point. Yeah, I could tell you're interested. That's one thing I like about you—you don't seem to be the type to play games. What you see is what you get. That's really refreshing, I have to tell you. So many women play these games—warm one minute, cold the next. They're really into you one day, totally avoiding you the next. It drives me crazy!"

As Josh went on and on about women and their games, she realized something. He wasn't emotionally available. Josh had withdrawn from taking risks in relationships. He was locked into the past, reliving his negative history with women. He couldn't see Kelly, the woman in front of him. He saw her only through the filter of his prior experiences. She let him wind down, then yawned and said it was past her bedtime. He thanked her for the conversation and they hung up. There was no request for another date and it didn't surprise her. *Next!* She thought, smiling to herself. *This is getting really fun and easy. All you have to do is pay attention, ask the right questions, and listen, and you find out all you need to know.*

✳ ✳ ✳

After Josh, Kelly took a short break from dating. She signed up for ballroom dance lessons with Marc and discovered a real passion. She went for lessons and attended the weekly evening dance party at the studio. Marc and Katrina's students traded partners throughout the evening. The tradition was for the men to approach the women and request a dance, and all of the guys knew to ask all of the women. This was completely different than those high school dances where the guys left all but the most beautiful girls sitting along the wall. It was an absolute blast, more fun than Kelly had ever had in those smoky night club scenes with weird partners who only wanted to get her in a clutch on the slow dances. This was classy and upscale—most of the guys were married and with their wives. It felt clean and fun, with no expectations.

She continued her routine of quiet time every day for reflection, journaling, meditation, and prayer. She felt calm and at peace, her life clarifying with each new insight.

Kelly's Biggest Temptation: Round Three

It was a glorious Saturday morning. Kelly went for an invigorating walk, stopping at a coffee shop for her favorite: mocha latte with whipped cream. She sat outside with the morning paper on the table, but found her attention drawn to the world around her, especially the cute dog at the next table who demanded petting. She loved people watching and feeling the fresh air on her skin. She was happy and content, more so than she could ever recall.

Her cell phone rang; she didn't recognize the number on caller i.d. but picked up anyway. She almost dropped her coffee cup when she heard the voice.

"Kevin? What a surprise." She waited, feeling her heart rate pick up.

"I know you probably don't want to hear anything I have to say, but please, don't hang up."

She waited.

"Good." He sounded enormously relieved. "Kelly, could you meet me for lunch today? I know I don't deserve it, but please just see me for that brief time. Will you?"

Kelly took a moment to sort through her emotions. She wasn't exactly sure what the right thing to do was, but she decided that this might be an opportunity of some kind.

"You're right, Kevin. You don't deserve it, but I deserve the chance to say a few things to you. So, yes, I'll meet you, as long as we agree that I get to say whatever I want in the course of our conversation and you will stay and listen respectfully until I'm done talking."

Kevin agreed. He seemed willing to jump through hoops to please her. She felt good about asking up front for what she wanted instead of letting him set the agenda like the "old Kelly." They set a time and place and disconnected.

After hanging up, Kelly felt a surge of emotions, primarily anger. What was happening here? How dare he call her up after all the unbelievable heartbreak he'd put her through?

Part of her wanted to call back and cancel or just stand him up. Another, more rational part, instructed her to calm down and prepare. Kelly remembered Martha's coaching for times like this: self-care and preparation!

Kelly decided on yoga for self care, so she rushed to make the 10:00 a.m. class with her favorite instructor. An hour later, as she completed the final stretches, Kelly felt ten times better. The fog of anger and puzzlement was gone, replaced by a plan of action.

Back home, Kelly meditated and said her mantra. She asked for guidance to do whatever was in the highest and greatest good of all concerned. From Martha, Kelly had learned that long-term happiness is founded on attention to the entire context of one's life, not on a myopic, selfish point of view. *If it makes you feel temporarily good, but hurts you in the long run, odds are it's an addictive choice. If it makes you feel good but everyone else bad, think again. Good life choices are cause for celebration not only in your life but in the lives that you touch.*

Afterward, Kelly wrote notes, carefully organizing them into bulleted points on an index card that she tucked into her bag. Last, she showered, letting the steaming water melt away the last of her anxiety. She blew her hair dry in a long, shiny style, and put on just enough makeup to accentuate her almond shaped eyes and give her lips a hint of color. She dressed in one of her favorite weekend outfits with sleek lines and just the right punch of color. Looking at herself in the mirror, she saw a strong, self-confident young woman, beautiful on the outside with the light of clarity shining from the inside. She was ready.

Kelly's notes:

- Make it clear we're here to talk, not hook up again, and that honesty is the goal

- Ask about his past; look for a pattern; face the reality

- Ask about his divorce: how is his ex doing:

- Stay focused on the big picture and core values, not just selfish desires

- No rescuing the wounded guy

- Let go of the outcome, get the truth on the table, and make decisions based on the reality; no fantasizing!

✳ ✳ ✳

Kelly deliberately arrived ten minutes late so she could knock Kevin's eyes out as she approached the table. It worked. He jumped up and pulled out her chair for her, something he'd rarely done when they were together.

"You look amazing." Kevin couldn't take his eyes off her. She thanked him for the compliment but remained carefully detached.

"Thank you for meeting me. I know I don't deserve it after the way I treated you."

"You're right, you don't. So, what is the purpose of this meeting?" Kelly was all business.

"Let's order first. How about a glass of wine?"

"No, Kevin. This is not a date. If that's what you had in mind, we're finished here." She started to rise. Kevin begged her to stay, assuring her that he would get to the point. Slowly, she sat down, waiting.

He took a breath, then plunged in. "The thing is, Kelly, I couldn't stop thinking about you. I know you probably find this hard to believe, but I really do love you. I've missed you so much." Tears moistened his eyes.

He explained that he and Lisa were separated and the papers filed for divorce. Yes, he missed his children every day and saw them as much as possible. He was ready to get on with his life; there was just one thing missing: Kelly.

He stopped at that point, pulling out a small black velvet box. He put it in front of her on the table.

"Kelly, I want you to know how serious I am. Please accept this as a symbol of my love for you." He opened the box and her eyes widened as she took in the incredible ring displayed there. It was a platinum band that sparkled with tiny inset diamonds, supporting an enormous princess cut center diamond—probably three carats in all. Kevin lifted Kelly's left hand and slipped the ring on before she could clear the buzzing in her head. She watched the dazzle of light reflecting from the jewelry on her finger, completely at a loss for words.

Kevin stroked her hand as he talked about how much he wanted a life with her. Slowly, she emerged from the fog in her head and excused herself for a powder room break.

Standing in the stall, mind reeling, she took several deep breaths. Her heart rate gradually slowed. Suddenly, Martha's voice popped into her head. *Grand romantic statements do not a relationship make, Kelly. Real love is in the day-to-day small gestures that endear you to one another and that solidify your commitment. Consistency, honesty, devotion, and being there for you—these are the things that show you a man loves you, not the size of the diamond he gives you.*

Kelly pulled her notes out and reviewed them. The fog lifted. She had clarity of thought and purpose. She was ready to have her say and let the chips fall. She looked down at the ring once more with longing. *Too bad,* she thought. *It really is a great ring!*

> *"Grand romantic statements do not a relationship make. Consistency, honesty, devotion, and being there for you—these are the things that show you a man loves you, not the size of the diamond he gives you."*

Back at the table, Kelly sat, looked at Kevin, and asked if he was ready to listen. "Of course. I'm sure you have a lot to say. Take your time—I'm not going anywhere." *We'll see about that,* she thought.

"First of all, I have some questions. It's important for you to be honest with me. My answer to you is dependent on it." She looked him directly in the eye for a moment, trying to convey her seriousness and to convince him that she'd know it if he lied to her.

Kevin looked a bit intimidated but held his own. "I have nothing to lose and everything to gain. If answering your questions is important to you, I'm here to do that."

Kelly took a breath and fired the first missile. "How many times before me did you cheat on Lisa?"

His face drained of color and his eyes darted away. He cleared his throat. He fidgeted. Finally, he looked back at her and answered. "Twice. Once when we were in college still dating and again when she was pregnant with our second child. They weren't important, Kelly, not relationships like you and I had."

"So this woman you had an affair with while Lisa was pregnant was unimportant to you. How does *she* feel about that?"

"Why are you doing this? That's ancient history. You must really hate me to harp on my past mistakes like this." The old self-centered Kevin reared his head again.

"If you can't take the heat, then we have nothing more to discuss." She felt utterly centered and grounded. She was ready for him to leave; she expected it in fact.

> *Tip: "Stay calm; women lose their power when they erupt in anger."*

He backed down. "I'm sorry. I have no right to say something like that after the way I hurt you."

"That's right," she said in an even tone of voice. She was careful to stay calm. *Women lose their power when they erupt in anger, Kelly.* Martha's coaching came to her at just the right moment.

"Of course she meant something to me, Kelly. I'm not a heartless S.O.B."

"And where is she today, this woman who meant so much to you?"

"I don't know. I broke up with her and lost touch. It's been years. I know it doesn't sound good, but I didn't love her the way I do you. You're the love of my life, Kelly. It's different, and it has been from the very beginning."

"Is there anyone else, Kevin? I need you to put *everything* on the table."

He looked positively pasty at this point. "Yes, one more. I had a one-night stand with a girl at the office before I met you. It was stupid and I regret it. There it is. Now you know it all."

Her gut told her that the truth was on the table. *Great*, she thought. *It's a pattern, just like Martha said it might be.*

"And what about Lisa, Kevin? Where is she in all of this?"

"We spent the past few months in therapy. It didn't work. We're on the same page about the divorce. It's for the best."

"Why didn't it work, Kevin?"

"What?"

"The counseling; why didn't it work?"

He sighed and looked away. "She couldn't get past my relationship with you. She didn't trust me and didn't believe she ever could. Honestly, Kelly, I think she knew I was still in love with you."

"So, was Lisa the one who called it quits?"

"Yes. But I would have eventually."

Kelly looked at her notes in her lap. *This is not really very flattering*, she thought. *The old me would have thought that all this meant something. Now, it just smells funny.*

"What kind of emotional shape is she in? Is she happy, moving forward?"

"She's angry, bitter and resentful toward me. I hope that with time, she'll get over it."

"*Get over it?* How does a woman get over losing her husband and the father of her children? How does a woman *get over* having her most cherished dreams smashed?" Kelly was astounded at Kevin's insensitivity.

"I didn't mean that the way it sounded." He looked unhappy. "This isn't going at all the way I thought it would." He sounded like a hurt little boy. Kelly resisted the impulse to soothe him and forged on.

She opened up, talked about the despair that had consumed her when their relationship first began, how long it took to recover from the breakup. Then she told him how devastated she'd been when

Kevin called her with Lisa on the phone listening. She spoke matter-of-factly, taking care to not dramatize. To his credit, Kevin's eyes misted again.

Then Kelly dropped the bombshell.

"Since we've been apart, I've done a great deal of soul-searching, and I've come to the realization that I had no business being with you. I now understand the agony that Lisa suffered and I realize that I contributed to that by sleeping with her husband. No, wait," she said, holding up her hand as Kevin tried to interrupt.

"I had no right to a relationship with another woman's husband, no matter what he said or did. I can only hope that this doesn't come back to haunt me some day. I've certainly earned some karmic payback.

"I also realized that I made it impossible for you to work things out with your wife, and for that I am truly sorry. I had no right to be intimate with you, knowing that you would lie to her, thereby destroying her trust in you.

"Lastly, and this hurts most of all, I contributed to a situation wherein your children have to grow up in a splintered family. I only wish I could make amends to them, and to Lisa. Of course, it would never be appropriate for me to approach her with this, so I have to settle for telling you and hoping that they can recover someday, somehow." Kelly's eyes filled with tears.

Kevin looked shattered. Tears ran down his face and he shook silently with sobs.

"Can you forgive me?" Kelly asked, tears running down her face.

"There's nothing to forgive you for. I'm the one who screwed up. I'm so sorry. I wish I had divorced years ago and been single when I met you. Oh God, what a mess I've made." He blew his nose and wiped his eyes. "Kelly, please forgive me for pulling you into the wreckage of my life, for hurting you, and for leaving you, not once but twice."

They sat quietly for a few minutes, sniffling and pulling themselves together. At that moment, she felt closer to him than ever. His armor had cracked, he was vulnerable, and for the first time, truly remorseful for hurting her.

Kevin raised her hand, turning it slowly so the ring caught the light, gazing at it. He looked so young and vulnerable, as if the pain had washed away his adult mask. He kissed her hand slowly, closing his eyes. She knew this would be their best moment, that there was no place left to go together.

Kelly forced herself to look ahead, into the future and what life might be like with Kevin. She forced herself to consider the whole picture, not just the "Kevin and Kelly" part. There was only one choice here, the only one that was truly the right choice. *In the highest and greatest good*, she thought.

Kelly's eyes filled with tears again as she spoke. "I can't be happy with you, Kevin. There are too many other lives at stake and I have no place in them. I can't imagine being fulfilled with you knowing that my presence in your life rubs salt in Lisa's wounds. I can't imagine feeling good about seeing your children when I'm the woman who took their father out of their home. I can't picture being truly joyful about the birth of our children together when your first three children suffer every day because of their parents' divorce, knowing that I helped make that happen.

"Yes," she said as Kevin tried to protest, "I did, Kevin. You know I did. I'm an adult. You didn't seduce some naïve teenager into an affair. I can't live with myself going forward if I don't take responsibility. And truthfully, I don't think I could ever really feel safe with you. Your pattern of running to other women when the going gets tough is something that may take years for you to break, if you ever do. I'm not willing to gamble with my life and my future children's lives while you work on that."

Kelly paused, feeling an ache in her heart that she hoped would someday pass. She realized Kevin was a soul mate of sorts, someone whose presence in her life had altered her, changed her forever. But Martha had explained that there are many, many potential soul mates in this world for each person, and that not all of them are right for us to walk through life with.

Kevin sat quietly, looking thoughtful and sad. He held Kelly's hand tightly, as if he knew that it was the last time.

"It's your life and you must do what you choose, but I can see that you're miserable. I'm immensely proud of you right now because I see the real man in you, maybe for the first time ever. I hope you'll keep that part of you alive.

"You're not ready for another relationship, Kevin. Even though you and Lisa may go ahead and divorce, you're tied to her for the rest of your life because of your children. Take your time. Focus on them. Make amends to Lisa, and understand that it may take a long time for her to forgive you. Make it right with your first family, before you seek a new one. You'll never feel okay with yourself until you earn the right to have a new family."

Kevin absorbed her words and slowly nodded. When he looked up again, his eyes were clear. "You're right. I don't like it and it won't be any fun, but you're right—I have some work to do as a co-parent with Lisa. Dating is too much right now, for me and especially for her and the kids. I've spent too much of my life focusing on me, on my own needs. It's time for me to focus on someone else's." Here his eyes looked sad again. "I hoped that would be you, Kelly, but marrying me really isn't a good deal for you."

They sat for a while longer, reminiscing about special times they'd shared, laughing. He insisted she keep the ring but she refused. Looking ahead, she couldn't imagine wearing Kevin's ring and explaining it to her future love, even if it was on her right hand. What if her future fiancé couldn't afford such a glorious ring? No, it simply wasn't appropriate for her to keep it.

Kelly hugged and kissed Kevin good-bye, wishing him the best, forcing her face to be bright and cheerful. In her car, she cried all the way home.

That night, Kelly called Martha. "It was by far the hardest thing I've ever done. I really love Kevin. But I realize that love is not enough to make a lifetime of joy. Letting go of him is the best thing, and I'm proud of myself for doing it." Martha applauded the courage it took to make the decision.

As she fell asleep that night, Kelly reflected on the day. *My mantra really worked*, she thought. Though she didn't know the future, she felt calm and peaceful in the certainty that all was working out for the best, for her highest and greatest good.

The Tenth Temptation:

Sacrificing Authenticity

Chapter Ten

Two weeks later Kelly jumped back into the dating scene. She took her time, pacing the timing and length of meetings with someone new. She interviewed them carefully, reflecting later and relying on her judgment. Periodically, she took a few weeks off from dating, focusing on friends and dancing.

For the first time, Kelly was in no hurry to meet "the one." She trusted that her life was unfolding exactly as it should. At the same time, she felt open in heart and spirit, ready to love and be loved, confident that she could be a good mate. She trusted herself to choose wisely this time.

Martha instructed her to consciously seek out happy couples and inquire about their stories. Kelly noted the men with wedding rings that she met in her business circles, particularly the ones who seemed stable and happy. When given the opportunity, she chatted with them about their families, careful to frame her questions so there wasn't even a hint of flirtation. What she discovered was eye-opening.

Almost all of the long-term married men that Kelly spoke to glowed when they talked about their wives. "She's the best thing that ever happened to me" was a frequent comment, as well as "I sure married up!" and "I thank God every day that I found her." On and on the conversations went as she prompted them for more: how they met, how he knew she was "the one," how he proposed. Per Martha's coaching, Kelly drank in the stories, affirming over and over that there were many, many good worthy men, and many, many happy marriages.

What an entirely new perspective! Kelly realized that she'd relied far too heavily on negative stories of love gone wrong from her single girl friends. While the stories were factually true, and she listened and empathized, they had poisoned her perspective, leaving her jaded.

Kelly's friends commented on her serenity. Though they didn't understand the change, they agreed it was for the better.

✻ ✻ ✻

Kelly sipped a mocha latte, sitting al fresco at a coffee shop. Her business trip over, she savored a rare Seattle fair weather day before driving to the airport. The tables were full. A guy approached and politely asked for one of her chairs. She looked up into a handsome face with warm brown eyes. Spontaneously, she invited him to join her.

"Hi, I'm Brian," he said, shaking her hand. As he sat, she noticed his tall, lean body, and how good his hand felt. She noted the small crinkles next to his eyes. *This man smiles a lot*, she thought. Her eyes flashed to his left hand—no ring.

Suddenly shy, Kelly smiled over her cup of coffee, as Brian led the conversation. He lived in Seattle, had for several years. Kelly hid her disappointment. *No long distance relationships*, she reminded herself. Still, it was fun to sit and chat for a while.

Brian was traveling as well, and they were mutually astonished to discover that they were booked on the same flight to Dallas. They shared a taxi to the airport, chatting the entire time, all the way through security and to their seats. Brian persuaded another traveler to switch seats so they could sit together.

Their conversation flowed. They had many things in common: music, books, and art. Just before their descent into DFW, Brian asked Kelly if he could take her out to dinner while he was in town. Disappointed but determined, Kelly declined. "I don't date long distance."

He didn't seem the least bit put off. "How about we go out to dinner as friends? No expectations, just dinner." His earnest eyes held Kelly's and his disarming smile tugged at her heart. She changed her mind.

"Just dinner then. I'll meet you there. This is not a date," she reiterated. Brian agreed. Still, Kelly had the distinct feeling that this was a man who knew what he wanted and didn't stop until he got it.

That night over dinner, Kelly and Brian talked as if they'd known each other for years. They shared the CNN version of their life stories. Brian was divorced with no kids. When queried about the how and why of his divorce, he withdrew a bit emotionally, a pained look on his face. He answered thoughtfully.

"Some of what happened in my marriage is very personal to my ex. I don't think she would want me telling her part of the story, especially to someone I don't yet know very well."

Her respect for Brian surged. He didn't speak disparagingly of the women in his past. He briefly described two people unable to find equilibrium. While the divorce was painful, it was mutual and inevitable, acknowledged by both as the right thing to do.

At the end of the evening, Kelly carefully maintained physical distance between them. She held out her hand to shake and Brian responded in kind, his eyes twinkling. Driving home, she wished he lived in Dallas. Something about him felt unique and different, special in a way she couldn't put her finger on. Later, she called Martha.

"It feels like I passed up a huge opportunity, Martha. Is that the right choice? Maybe if we date for a while and it goes really well, he'll decide to move here."

"Could you see yourself moving there, Kelly?"

"Not really. I have so many friends here and I can't imagine being so far away from my family. But we could work all that out later, right? It's not like we have to figure out our whole lives right now, is it? What's wrong with keeping my mouth shut and seeing what develops?"

Temptation: Sacrificing Authenticity

"Good question, Kelly. You tell me. What would it be like for you to date this guy with him living there and you here? Imagine days and sometimes weeks going by without seeing him. Picture yourself wondering if he's ever going to move here."

Kelly felt a knot in the pit of her stomach. "It doesn't feel good at all."

"And what about the honeymoon effect that long distance couples experience? Are you willing to stake your whole future on feelings that you can't verify through day-to-day real life experience?"

Martha paused, then added softly, "Are you willing to take that much risk, Kelly?"

"No, I'm not," she answered, sighing. "No matter how special he is, the fact is that he lives in another city. For me, that would be endlessly frustrating."

"What kind of relationship would it be if you spoke up about your frustration? Even more important, what kind of relationship would it be if you didn't speak up?"

Kelly sighed again. "Not good. But he's so wonderful, or he seems to be. What's wrong with letting a bond develop first, then tackle the issue? Won't he have a bigger incentive to move here to be with me if he falls in love first?"

"Kelly, you're right at the heart of the **Tenth Temptation:** *sacrificing authenticity* to get the guy. This is where the rubber meets the road in a manner of speaking. It's one thing to talk about what you really want; it's another to be adamant about your vision of life in the face of a great guy who's *almost* right for you. Once again you are presented with that fatal flaw in the relationship that sets you up for anxiety.

"When starting a new relationship with a huge red flag, we're strongly tempted as women to keep our mouths shut, to accept the situation silently, and to segue into wishful thinking. All with the goal of getting the guy—the absolute worst goal you can set! Sounds strange to say that, doesn't it, when the goal is a relationship?"

> *"It's easy to talk about what you really want. But remaining adamant about your vision of life in the face of a great guy who's almost right for you demands an enormous amount of willpower."*

"All I know is that when I lock onto a certain guy and think he's 'the one,' I stop looking at the whole picture. Plus it starts to feel false and insincere. I can't really speak my mind because there's this elephant in the room—the red flag issue I'm hoping will go away." Kelly sighed again. This was hard, harder than she'd anticipated.

"When you accept something unacceptable, you take away your authentic voice, Kelly. This one trumps all the others—every temptation we've discussed. If you are authentic, everything has a way of sorting out. If you are not, everything gets chaotic and confused—a poor foundation for a relationship."

Martha paused, then gently asked, "What does your gut tell you is the right thing to do?"

Though she felt immensely disappointed, Kelly affirmed the truth. "It tells me to let this go. I won't gamble my future on wishful thinking. He's not available and that, unfortunately, is that.

> "When you accept something unacceptable, you take away your authentic voice. This one trumps all the others - every temptation we've discussed. If you are authentic, everything has a way of sorting out."

"I know myself well enough to know that if I fall in love with him long distance, I won't have the patience to wait and pace the relationship, hoping he'll want to move here. I don't want to feel frustrated and sorry for myself down the road. I'd rather say no today than 'what a waste of my time!' in a couple of years."

✼ ✼ ✼

Over the next few weeks, Kelly's dating life took an interesting turn. Suddenly, she had two different guys pursuing her. One, Greg, was a pilot, divorced for four years with two children. He seemed enchanted with Kelly. He was attractive but she wasn't quite sure of her feelings. She accepted three dates and felt a few sparks fly by the end of the third date. Though mature, Greg was a little egotistical in some way she couldn't quite identify.

Meanwhile, Steve was also in pursuit. At forty three, he had never been married. *What's wrong with him?*, Kelly couldn't help thinking. He was cute but a little emotionally distant and difficult to connect with. *We'll see*, she thought.

Then Brian called. "I'm coming to Dallas next week and wondered if we could get together for dinner."

She hesitated, torn between wanting to see him again and knowing that it couldn't possibly go anywhere. He quickly reassured her that he understood they weren't dating. Still, there was an unmistakable attraction between them. She accepted and they made plans.

At dinner, they picked up where they'd left off just three weeks earlier. The time flew by. Two and a half hours later, their conversation trailed off as both slowly realized that the evening was almost over. Brian gazed steadily at Kelly as he picked up her hand and briefly ran his thumb over her skin. He smiled and so did she. He was quiet, as though he had something to say but the timing wasn't right.

At Kelly's car, they hugged briefly. She disengaged quickly, thanking him for dinner. As she drove away, she saw him in her rear view mirror, leaning against his car, arms folded, smiling at her. Warmth invaded her heart and body. Being around Brian did that. *Too bad*, she thought, feeling the missed opportunity. Still, she was proud of her resolve. Deep down, she knew that she couldn't possibly date this amazing man long distance. *Nope*, she thought, *I'd want this guy up close and frequent!* She forced herself once again to let go of Brian, trusting that if it was meant to be, something would change.

Kelly went out with Greg again. That evening, she found herself comparing Greg with Brian, her feelings for Greg with her feelings for Brian. There was no contest.

Later, Kelly shared her revelation with Martha. "I realized that the way I felt wasn't about Brian—it was about me. The feelings I have when I see Brian are the feelings that I want to feel with a guy, and I don't want anything less than that. With Greg, something's missing and what matters is that I don't waste my time."

Kelly reflected on her feelings for Steve and came to the same conclusion: *something's missing and I don't need to figure it out.* Steve seemed to arrive at the same conclusion, as he didn't call or ask her out again. *Great!* Kelly thought. *Next!*

Brian called one night. Martha had warned her that long conversations over the phone with an unavailable guy can provoke fantasies, so she cut it short at half an hour. Brian asked her for dinner for his next trip in two weeks and she declined. "This can't go anywhere. I'm attracted to you but I need to be available to meet someone I can share my life with, and you're not here to do that." He said he understood. There was a hint of sadness in their goodbye that night. *Well, that's the end of that*, she thought.

Kelly moved forward but dating lurched to a halt. No one called, no one emailed. Her candidates dwindled to zero. It was okay; in fact it was great. Kelly enjoyed her life. Work was fun—her business was growing and clients constantly expressed appreciation for her work.

Her spiritual life continued to grow. Her daily practices of meditation and prayer brought her astonishing clarity and peace of mind.

* * *

Kelly woke slowly, stretching and wiggling her toes. Trixie pounced on them. She smiled and sat up to pet her. It was Saturday in early September, a beautiful morning. Something tickled in the back of her mind about the date but she was too sleepy to make sense of it.

Later, a surprise waited for Kelly in the lobby of her building—a gorgeous mixed bouquet of lavender and butter yellow tulips. The message on the card read:

> *Kelly,*
> *Lovely flowers for a lovely woman. I hope to see you soon.*
> *Brian*

As she opened her door, the phone rang. She picked up and greeted Brian. "What a surprise! How are you?" She couldn't help but feel a thrill of delight at the sound of his voice.

"Kelly, listen, I know we said no more dates, but I hope you'll make an exception. It's important—I have some news to share with you. May I treat you to dinner Friday night?"

She accepted, following her gut. After hanging up, she wondered what his news was about. Suddenly, her heart dropped. Maybe he'd met someone else in Seattle. Immediately, she wondered why that would bother her. After all, hadn't she turned him down repeatedly?

That evening as she sat on her sofa petting Trixie, she remembered the significance of the date. One year ago today she'd started the program with Martha! She flipped through her journal, re-reading certain pages, smiling and shaking her head. Later, she called Martha.

"This is odd," she said. "Here I am beaming about my progress over the past year, yet I still don't have the guy, the ring, or the rest of it!" Kelly laughed at the paradox of her life. Happy, content, and even joyful—yet still single.

"I'm so glad to hear that you're permanently re-wired to care for yourself and realize your potential as a woman, to make wise choices and invest in long-term outcomes.

"The program isn't over yet, so get ready. When women reach this point in their lives it's as if a powerful message goes out to the universe that says 'I'm ready!' and an answer always comes back. I don't know what yours will be or the timing of it, but isn't it exciting anticipating it?"

Kelly thanked Martha for her support and coaching. Later, she lit a candle and said a special prayer of gratitude. It was a powerful full-circle moment in her life and she felt it down to her toes.

✳ ✳ ✳

Friday night, Kelly arrived at the restaurant with butterflies in her stomach. Walking in, she spotted Brian standing by the bar with a martini in his hand talking to a striking blond. She stopped and watched, her heart plummeting to the floor. Brian talked animatedly; the blond laughed at something he said, reaching out to touch his arm.

Wonderful, Kelly thought dismally. *I chased him off and now he's hooked up with someone else!*

She stopped in the ladies room, taking time for a little inner dialogue. *Okay, so he's got someone else. What did you expect? Get over it. Be a real friend and go out there and congratulate him.*

Holding her head high, she marched out of the restroom. She pasted on her brightest smile and approached Brian and Blondie, stubbornly ignoring her rapidly beating heart and sweaty palms.

"Hi, Brian. How are you?" she asked, a bit stiffly. She turned to Blondie and thrust out her hand.

"I'm Kelly."

"It's so nice to meet you, Kelly. I'm Evelyn," said Blondie, shaking her hand warmly and smiling. "I've heard so many good things about you," she added, cutting her eyes to Brian with an impish grin.

He shot Evelyn a warning look. She smiled but said no more. Brian turned to Kelly and hugged her warmly, telling her their table would be ready soon.

For the next agonizingly long ten minutes, Kelly chatted with Brian and Evelyn. Her head buzzed slightly and she was confused. So far, no announcement of who Blondie was in Brian's life.

Suddenly, Evelyn looked at her watch and declared she was late. She hugged Brian, kissing him on the cheek, told Kelly again how nice it was to meet her, and left. Kelly was astonished. *What is going on here?*

Brian escorted her into the dining room, pulling out her chair. They perused the wine and dinner menu, ordered something—Kelly had no idea what. She couldn't quite clear the fog in her head. *Might as well dive in and get it over with*, she thought.

"She's just lovely, Brian. Where did you meet her?" Kelly asked abruptly.

"Huh? Oh, you mean Evelyn? We met at an industry conference."

"Well, that's just great. Is she a Dallas girl?"

"Dallas girl? Uh, yeah, she lives in Dallas."

"That's nice." Sarcasm leaked into Kelly's voice. Brian looked confused. "So why exactly am I here tonight?" She hated herself for the venom in her voice but was powerless to control it.

Brian looked genuinely puzzled.

"What? Oh, I guess this is a bit confusing. I mean, you did make it clear that you don't do long distance relationships, and I respect that. But I wanted to tell you some…"

"Yeah, I get it," Kelly bit off. "But why send me flowers and take me to dinner just to tell me you're in love with Evelyn?"

Now Brian looked totally flummoxed. His forehead wrinkled and his head tilted as he looked at Kelly. Then he laughed out loud.

"What? You thought…I mean, oh, Kelly!" He laughed and sputtered. Kelly fumed.

"Don't think this means something, Brian. And quit laughing at me! What are you…?" she stopped as Brian took her hand and kissed it. "What's Blondie going to say about this?" she asked lamely, her stomach fluttering.

"Blondie? You mean Evelyn? I'm sure she'd be thrilled to hear that I'm kissing your hand." Brian smiled.

"Listen for a minute, Kelly. I've known Evelyn for years. *We are just friends.* There's never been any more to it than that."

Kelly's heart rate slowed down and her anger evaporated.

"I asked you here to tell you I'm moving to Dallas at the end of the month. I wanted you to know because you're one of the reasons for my decision. You're not the only reason," he added hastily. "I don't want you to feel pressured."

Kelly felt like she was on a roller coaster. Her emotions couldn't adjust this quickly. One minute, Brian's introducing her to another woman. The next, he's moving to Dallas! She took a deep breath.

"As you know, my family lives here. I didn't emphasize the importance of that because I wasn't sure whether I wanted to move back. Life is very different since I moved to Seattle eight years ago, and I didn't think I'd ever want to move back. But things change." He smiled at her and it finally sunk in: *Brian is moving to Dallas!*

His family—parents and sister with two children—constantly nagged him about moving back and he'd thought about it, but he had a life in Seattle. Then, he'd met Kelly, and the idea of moving back became more appealing. He went to his CEO and worked out a change.

Kelly listened, astonished. He paused nervously and asked her to say something. She took a deep breath and chose her words carefully.

"Brian, I'm really excited that you're moving here, but what if we date and it doesn't work out between us?"

"First of all, I can't imagine that," he said with a grin. "But that's a risk I'm prepared to take. The worst that happens is that I live close to my family again. I'm doing this for me, Kelly. You're a big part of the equation, no doubt about it, but you're not responsible for my choice." He lifted her hand to his lips and slowly kissed it, gazing into her eyes. "I mean, what kind of idiot would let you get away?"

Kelly melted inside but didn't surrender her resolve. "That sounds wonderful, Brian. But I barely know you. Just because you're moving here doesn't mean we'll suddenly spend a ton of time together, at least not right away. I prefer pacing things slowly."

Brian smiled and assured her he understood. "I'm a patient guy. You need to find out who I really am—you *should* do that—before you give your heart. I have time." He grinned at her again with a confident look that spoke volumes.

Kelly didn't stop there. "There's one more thing, Brian. Let's take a few weeks to get to know each other better before we decide to be exclusive." Kelly knew she didn't have anyone else on her radar, but he didn't need to know that.

"I can handle that. Just so you know, though, I'm not interested in anyone else right now. My focus is on you." He smiled again, eyes twinkling. The butterflies danced in Kelly's stomach but she mentally shushed them.

The rest of dinner was wonderful. As always, their conversation flowed easily. Kelly took the opportunity to ask more questions about Brian's background, carefully working in ways to clarify his past behavior and character. He passed with flying colors. Later, standing at Kelly's car and saying goodnight, Brian kissed her for the first time. It was warm and slow, and absolutely delicious. She felt her knees wobble. She pulled away, said good night and drove away. *Mercy me, it won't be easy to pace this one*, she thought.

Kelly recalled Martha's coaching. *The goal is healthy passion for a lifetime, not a brief hot fling. If it's worth having, it's worth pacing because your odds of success are much, much higher.*

This guy is definitely worth it, Kelly thought as she drove home. *No way am I going to risk screwing it up by rushing in.* She smiled to herself. For the first time ever, she felt confident and in control of herself. She sensed

> "The goal is healthy passion for a lifetime, not a brief hot fling. If it's worth having, it's worth pacing because your odds of success are much, much higher."

her original assessment of Brian would prove accurate. Still, *we'll see*, she said silently.

✳ ✳ ✳

The next three months flew by. Kelly and Brian saw each other two to three times every week, gradually spending more time together, more frequently. They went to brunch, dinner, and the movies. They attended plays, concerts, and the symphony. Per Martha's coaching, Kelly guided their choice of venues to avoid intimate evenings at one of their homes. *If you want to put off sex, you must avoid situations that create temptation.*

About three weeks into their relationship, Kelly discussed sex with Brian, explaining her decision to wait at least six months. Brian shocked her by revealing he had a timeline as well. "Don't get me wrong," Brian said, grinning. "I would love to make love to you today. But I've learned it doesn't make sense to take that step until I know exactly where I stand. There's too much at stake. Besides, like I said, I'm a patient man." The look he gave her made her skin tingle.

> *Tip: "Avoid intimate, romantic situations and settings that create temptation if you want to put off sex."*

Too Good to be True?

Kelly was having the best dating time of her life. She and Brain laughed together, kissed passionately (but nothing more for now), read books together, went for long walks, and enjoyed every moment together. It was almost too good to be true.

It was time to set the stage for the long haul, so she chose her timing at dinner one night and brought up the subject. Kelly told Brian that she viewed dating as a purposeful search for a life mate. "While we're still getting to know each other and exploring our feelings, I need to know if that's what you're looking for—marriage and lifetime love. I'm not interested in dating for fun and games with no strings attached."

Brian hesitated before speaking. "One of the things I like about you is your honesty—you really put it on the line. I feel honored that you would consider me as a potential husband. This is not a fling for me, Kelly. I feel closer to you every day—you are becoming a very important part of my life. But marriage is a huge step, and a scary one for me. I've failed at it once and it was the most painful thing I've ever been through. I have to be honest and tell you that I'm not sure I can do it again."

There it was, on the table, the one thing Kelly most dreaded hearing—Brian was afraid of marriage. Her heart sank. They both found little to say the rest of the evening. Kelly avoided kissing Brian goodnight. "Kelly," he said softly. "I'm so sorry I disappointed you. Please, let's talk about it." She begged for time to think over their conversation, promising to discuss it later. Then she called Martha.

"This is just like all the men in the past," she said, feeling tears sting her eyes. "I don't know what to do. Should I just end it now and spare myself the pain of rejection later? Brian is so special, so wonderful in all the ways I've always dreamed of. But he doesn't want what I want. Oh Martha, what do I do?"

"What are your choices?"

Pushing him to state a stronger intention would put her in the lead in the relationship, so that wasn't an option. She didn't want to play games by dating other men to provoke jealousy and a false commitment. So they agreed that her only viable choices were: a.) Continue dating Brian and hope that he had a change of heart down the road; or b.) Break up now, citing the difference in their intentions. Martha recommended sleeping on the decision for a couple of nights since Kelly seemed so torn.

Over the next three days, she felt hurt and sad, then irritated and upset. After three nights of restless sleep and three days of meditation and prayer, she finally felt calm and resolute. Honesty, she decided, was the best path. They had plans for dinner that night so she called and suggested a quiet venue.

After some small talk, she launched in. "I want to continue our discussion from the other night, Brian. Thank you for being so honest with me. That's one of the things I appreciate about you. I want to ask you something but before I do, please know that hearing the

truth, no matter how much it might hurt, is very important to me."
He quickly assured her that whatever it was, he'd answer honestly.

"Okay. What I need to know is this—are you telling me you're
afraid of marriage because I'm not the right person for you? Maybe
I'm Ms. Right Now but not Ms. Right. I really need to know what
you feel about this, even if it's hard to tell me." Kelly was careful
to keep her voice neutral and curious without appearing fragile—no
trembling chin, no quavering voice. Martha had taught her that most
men will cut off their arms before deliberately hurting a woman's
feelings, making it vital to be strong when asking questions like this
one.

"No, absolutely not. My issue is with marriage, not with you.
You are everything I've looked for in a woman, Kelly. I'm very serious
about this relationship—I don't have any desire to look further." He
held her gaze and she saw nothing but truth in his eyes.

"Okay. But what is the point of dating and getting closer if we're
not moving toward the possibility of marriage? I don't want to live
with a man, Brian. That wouldn't be enough for me."

"I understand and respect that. I'm not sure," he said, looking
puzzled. "I have to admit I didn't think that far ahead. You're right,
though. There's not much point if marriage is what you want and I'm
not sure I can do it." His eyes held a sad look. "On the other hand, I
can't imagine not being with you, Kelly."

Their conversation continued from there, Brian reassuring her
that his feelings for her were real and growing stronger the better he
knew her. He also shared his fears about marriage, reiterating that it
was difficult for him to promise they were headed that way. She felt
the authenticity of his words but couldn't get a handle on how to
proceed. Finally, it dawned on her. *Just tell the truth, and let the chips
fall where they may.*

"Brian, this leaves me in an awkward position. There's only one
thing I can think of that feels right and that is to take a break from
seeing each other, maybe go back to dating other people. I don't want
you to think this is easy for me to do—because it's not. And I don't
want you to think I'm looking for a way out. You are the kind of guy
I always hoped to meet and I really don't want to go back out there

looking again. But I can't see being comfortable with a dating path that isn't about exploring the possibility of marriage. With that off the table, I'll be far too anxious, always wondering where we're headed and fearful that you'll never change your mind. That's not my idea of a great start to a relationship for either of us. So, I think it's best for me to back off for now." Her eyes glistened with tears and so did his. Their goodbye was sad that night, even though Brian declared his intention to not give up on their relationship—this wasn't a breakup as far as he was concerned. Still, he offered no solutions.

✳ ✳ ✳

Two weeks dragged by. Brian sent emails with short, sweet messages like "I'm thinking of you" and "I miss you." She saved them but didn't respond. Oddly, she didn't feel tremendously sad, even though it looked like they were over.

She didn't have the heart for dating yet so she focused on work and spending time with friends. Every day, she said a little prayer asking for things to work out in both hers and Brian's greatest and highest good, whatever that might be. Using her mantra, she worked on letting go of her attachment to the end result, knowing it was out of her control.

Out of the blue, he called, begging her to meet him for dinner, asking her to wait until then to talk. She accepted with a mix of dread and anticipation. This could be their last contact and final goodbye.

✳ ✳ ✳

The minute Kelly saw Brian, her heart swelled. He was so cute, his smile so endearing. He was all smiles, holding her tightly as he hugged her.

Brian suggested a toast and they clinked glasses of wine as he said "to us." He took a sip and set down his glass.

"Kelly, I've come to a decision. Even though I'm still nervous about marriage, I'm absolutely certain about you. I want to be with you and I don't want anything standing in the way. So, I'm on the path of exploring marriage as a possibility with you. If you're still interested." His eyes twinkled.

Inwardly, she let out a huge sigh of relief. "I am, but I just want to make sure you're not doing this because you feel pressured." She studied his face, looking for any sign of evasion.

"I don't feel at all pressured. You told me the truth about where you stood and you took action to take care of yourself—I have complete respect for that." Brian gazed steadily at her, his clear eyes conveying nothing but the truth.

Kelly took the opportunity to go a little deeper, bringing up children. Brian assured her that children were a possibility, though they both acknowledged that nothing was guaranteed. Kelly stated firmly that her primary purpose was a healthy, loving relationship. "If that includes kids someday, that will be wonderful," she told Brian, "but I won't rush a relationship because of a ticking biological clock, even if that means I miss the opportunity to be a mom." Kelly and Martha's discussions on this subject were pivotal for her. Kelly was absolutely clear that the priority line-up was spiritual and self first, relationship second, and children only with the rest of the pieces in place.

Kelly and Brian agreed that if one of them had a change of heart, the other was to be immediately informed. Their commitment was to openness and honesty, no stringing along tolerated.

When Kelly discussed it later with Martha, her joy bubbled over. "It's amazing how it all works out just by being honest and letting go of the outcome." Martha asked what she learned about Brian through the experience. "What I see is that even though he's scared, he's so intentional that he's willing to work through his fears and keep stepping forward. So far, at least. I hope that's the real Brian. *We'll see*," she concluded, pulling herself back down to earth. She knew they'd just begun to really know one another.

Dating and Discovering

Later, they discussed in-depth their prior relationships. Kelly told Brian about her worst moments—dating Kevin, a married man, the remorse she felt, and the resolution of their relationship. Brian listened intently, asking how she felt about fidelity. Kelly's eyes teared as she told him how deeply meaningful it was to her. Yes, she'd been totally messed up about it in the past, but she got it now. Brian hugged her and assured her he admired her growth.

He shared more about his marriage. His ex-wife Cheryl hadn't shared the same values. He thought she would give up partying after married, focus on him and creating a life together, but she didn't. He grew angrier while she grew more defensive.

Finally, Brian threw in the towel. He felt guilty about giving up, but the struggle had been long and painful. The truth was that she was an alcoholic. Though she voiced her desire to recover, the changes were fleeting and never lasted. She hadn't fought the divorce, but he still viewed it as a failure. After all, he'd promised "till death."

Kelly admired his compassion and loyalty.

One Friday, Brian picked her up at 2:00 in the afternoon carrying a fully packed picnic basket. They spent the afternoon on a huge blanket spread on the grass at the Dallas Arboretum, a beautiful garden sanctuary, sipping wine, taking bites of cheese, crackers and other goodies, and gazing at each other. They couldn't stop talking and laughing. Brian stole a few public kisses. Kelly giggled like a teenager, looking around to see if anyone else saw them. The maintenance crew had to kick them out at the end of the day because they lost all sense of time.

Kelly made an amazing discovery. Never before had she been courted by a man. By flinging herself at men, she'd robbed herself of the glorious experience of being pursued by a worthy suitor.

She'd also deprived herself of the light-hearted, innocent stage of love that she and Brian shared. Martha was right: this was a totally new set of experiences. She heard Martha's words in her mind: *The early, innocent stage of love is joyous. Those memories are precious to draw upon as the years go by; they sustain you through difficult times that inevitably lie ahead. So many couples today bypass this stage by getting sexually and emotionally intense far too quickly.*

Kelly realized most of her prior boyfriends wouldn't have made it past her new screening process. That was eye-opening as well. The kind of guy who could, she realized, was the kind of guy she'd overlooked in the past—a guy with real character and emotional strength.

Brian called, asking her out in advance, never taking for granted that her time belonged to him. He made dinner reservations, bought tickets, and insisted on paying. "I'm lucky enough to spend time with you, Kelly. The least I can do is take care of the check."

Brian did what he committed to do. He called when he said, showed up on time or even a bit early, but never too early.

He gave Kelly sweet sentimental cards and often brought her flowers. He showed his loving nature in dozens of small ways. Never did he give extravagant gifts followed by heavy expectations. Kelly felt completely free to be herself and let things unfold. She felt secure in the knowledge of her own self-care and in the certainty of Brian's intentions. *So far, so good*, she thought. *"We'll see" is definitely turning into something wonderful!*

Brian insisted on celebrating the monthly anniversary of the day they met. Each month on the 12th, he gave her a card and one rose for every month together, though Kelly pointed out that there was a big gap between the day they met and the day they actually started dating. Brian said that didn't matter because as far as he was concerned, his life changed the day he met her. "You were in the back of my mind from day one," he told her. "I knew that something was different, even though I didn't yet know what it was."

On their sixth "anniversary" (three months of actual dating), he took her to dinner, giving her half a dozen red roses and a card. They discussed exclusivity and Kelly admitted that she hadn't dated anyone since he'd told her he was moving to Dallas. He smiled and said he knew that. She hit him playfully, and they laughed at her half-hearted attempt to hold him at bay.

That night, as Brian wrapped Kelly in his arms, he whispered in her ear. "I love you, Kelly. You don't have to say anything back yet. I just thought you might want to know that someone loves you." He kissed her again and walked away from her door whistling a little tune. That night, she called him and whispered, "Someone loves you, too!"

Kelly showed Brian how much she cared by giving back in small, romantic ways. She invited him over and cooked his favorite meal. She gave him cards. She listened and gave him advice about work issues. When clients gave her thank-you gifts like show tickets, she immediately called and invited him. She even surprised him one day with flowers.

Though she gave to Brian frequently and from the heart, Kelly carefully left the leading up to him. She resisted the temptation to call him and ask him out. She wanted to see how often he'd call without prompting from her. Never was she disappointed. After six weeks, Brian called daily, even if was just a short "how's your day going, sweetie?" When he traveled, he gave her his itinerary, calling her from the road daily.

Kelly was deeply in love. After careful self-diagnosis, she was certain. Symptom number one: she woke up thinking about Brian, she fell asleep thinking about him, and she walked around all day with a little smile thinking about him. Symptom number two: she had major flutters in her heart and stomach the moment the doorbell rang for their dates. Symptom number three: she couldn't clearly remember what life was like before him. It was as if his presence in her life had erased every prior bad relationship. She couldn't imagine life without him. They'd dated for almost nine months; it seemed like a flash and it seemed like forever.

Their relationship progressed so smoothly it was like a dream come true. They never argued, never had conflict. Martha laughed and reminded Kelly they were definitely in the enchantment phase of their relationship. "You'll eventually hit a rough patch of some kind. The good news is that you're building a strong foundation of mutual respect, love, and trust, and that should get you through just about anything."

Kelly discovered what real love was all about. Unlike the intense infatuations she'd experienced in the past, this love unfolded over time, gently entangling her life and Brian's in a warm circle of emotional security. This love grew deeper roots each day. There were none of the huge ups and down, the addictive cycles that characterized her past relationships.

For the first time in her life, Kelly understood what it was like to create emotional security with a man through adherence to the process, adherence to her values, and open, candid communication. Their relationship was perfectly balanced: they both wanted it, a lot, and it showed. They regularly expressed how grateful they were for finding each other.

✳ ✳ ✳

One year from the day Kelly and Brian met in Seattle, nine months after his move to Dallas, they had dinner at one of their favorite restaurants to celebrate their anniversary.

Brian seemed unusually agitated during their meal but Kelly couldn't coax him to explain. They left the restaurant and drove to a small, enchanting little park. The steps leading from the street to the park area were engraved with quotes from famous poets.

It was a beautiful evening in early June and stars shone brightly. They strolled hand in hand, reading the poetry out loud as they went. One of the many, many things Kelly loved about Brian was his enjoyment of literature. They read together frequently and Kelly relished the spirited dialogs that resulted.

They came to a bench and Brian drew Kelly down to sit with him. "Kelly, I want to give you your anniversary gift now," he told her. They'd planned a little celebration at her place later. Kelly's gift for Brian was at home, not here. Brian saw the flicker of concern on her face.

"Don't worry, we'll get to the rest later." He pulled a tiny black box with a little pink ribbon out of his pocket and handed it to her. Kelly's eyes widened and her heart beat faster. Slowly, she untied the ribbon and opened the box. Inside was a smaller velvet box. Her fingers shook so much she couldn't get it out. Brian did it for her, opening the velvet box and taking out the sparkling ring inside. He held it in his fingers, holding Kelly's hand, his eyes misting.

"This past year has been a dream come true for me. You're the love of my life and I can't imagine living even one day without you. Will you marry me?"

Kelly's eyes filled with tears as she blurted "Yes!" They hugged, both sniffling, and kissed. Brian guided the ring onto her finger. It was stunning. Tiny rubies framed a brilliant white diamond.

Her heart overflowed. She was amazed that Brian had managed to surprise her so completely. Though they'd shopped for rings and they'd discussed marriage, he'd still caught her wonderfully off-guard.

It was a magical night. Kelly only wished she could somehow slow time, make each moment last for hours. She already felt deeply loved and cherished. Tonight, their love seemed even deeper and more precious, if that was possible.

Beyond the Temptations:

Creating Real Love

Chapter Eleven

Kelly began eagerly planning their wedding. They'd set the date for the following June, on their second anniversary. Brian insisted on being involved, so they spent many hours talking to florists and caterers, considering various venues. When their opinions differed, he deferred to her, saying, "Marrying you is the whole point of the day for me, Kelly; nothing else matters as long as you're happy." He even took dance lessons with her, gamely signing up for private instruction so they could dance together at their wedding.

As Kelly met Brian's friends and colleagues she heard over and over how wonderful, kind and generous he was, how lucky she was to have him. Never did she hear even a hint of bad behavior; there were no stories about his womanizing days, no wink-wink from his male friends hinting at a colorful past. *How did I not see this before*, she wondered, *the importance of looking at a guy's past behavior, of paying attention to what his friends say about him?*

Some of her single friends expressed envy about Kelly's incredible "good luck" in finding Brian. She tried to explain that it wasn't luck at all, but her words fell flat. They didn't get it yet and she couldn't reveal the secret of overcoming the Temptations.

Martha coached Kelly in the next stage of establishing a good foundation for marriage. "Most couples treat engagement as if they're already married except for the paperwork. But engagement means you *want* to marry. It should be

> *"Engagement means you want to marry, not that you're already married except for the paperwork. You must be prepared to end a relationship right up to the moment you walk down the aisle if you realize it's not right for you."*

used to make certain that marrying is the right thing for both of you, and for your future children.

"Many couples who divorce early in a marriage report later that they *knew they were making a mistake on their wedding day* but they married anyway to avoid the embarrassment or the pain of a break-up. Many people would rather marry and divorce than deal with ending a long-term relationship that's not right for them. That happens in *non-intentional, unconscious* dating. You're dating intentionally, but there are still some steps," Martha concluded.

"As much as this flies in the face of popular thinking, you must be prepared to end this relationship right up to the moment you walk down the aisle if you realize it's not right. Are you willing to do that?"

Kelly thought about it carefully, realizing how critical this was. "Yes," she said slowly. "I would rather be embarrassed and deal with the grief of a break up than go through a divorce."

Following Martha's coaching, Kelly gained Brian's participation in setting specific intentions and goals for their marriage. They discussed everything from housework to children, careers, finances, and in-laws, avoiding the temptation to just go along. Each discussion strengthened their relationship, even when they disagreed about the small stuff. Overall, they affirmed that their values and direction in life were aligned. The wedding day approached and Kelly's excitement grew.

✳ ✳ ✳

Kelly's phone rang at 7:15 and she grabbed it, quickly answering. It was Brian, calling to apologize for being late and to tell her he would be a few more minutes. His voice sounded strange but Kelly assured him that it was okay. It wasn't at all like him to be late.

Thirty minutes later, Brian arrived. When Kelly opened the door, she could tell something was very wrong.

Panicking, Kelly drew him in, asking "What is it, Sweetheart? What happened? Are your parents okay, your sister?"

"No, no, Kelly, my family is fine—don't worry; everyone's okay. Can I um get a glass of water?"

When Kelly returned with his water, he was sitting on the sofa, his elbows propped on his knees, his head in his hands. She sat down slowly and waited.

Brian sighed, not looking up at her. He spoke slowly and painfully, sniffling occasionally.

"I got a call today from Cheryl's parents."

"She…she died; she overdosed on pills and alcohol." His shoulders shook with silent sobs. Kelly tried to hug him but he was stiff, unresponsive. Instead, she rested a supporting hand on his arm and waited for him to speak.

"They said she'd been in and out of treatment, never sticking with it. Then she seemed to be doing better, going to meetings. They went out of town, just for a few days, thinking she'd be okay. She looked and sounded fine when they left, but then…" he couldn't continue. "They found her when they got home. They're devastated, eaten up with guilt."

There it was. Kelly knew instinctively that Brian was referring to himself as well.

"Brian, I'm so sorry. Of course, you know that it's not their fault, don't you?"

"Of course! They're the best, most loving people in the world. They did all they could." He went quiet.

"I thought Cheryl was recovering. I thought that living with her parents, she'd stay on course. But now I don't know. Maybe if I hadn't left…

"Brian…"

"No, don't interrupt." His voice was distant, disconnected in a way she'd never heard before. "I don't know if I can go through with this, Kelly.

"It's not you. You're perfect; you're the best thing that's ever happened to me. I just…I'm not sure I can be a good husband. I failed so badly the first time. The truth is that I left her in her hour of need. I wasn't committed enough to stick it out, to help her with her recovery. *She was my wife, and I bailed!*

"Kelly, I can't do that to you—I don't want to let you down. That would kill me."

Kelly sat perfectly still. This wasn't happening. Their wedding was six weeks away, everything was planned. They were so happy.

Brian rambled on about his failure, wiping away the tears as he talked. Kelly's heart felt ripped from her chest. She tried to hold Brian, comfort him, tell him everything was going to be okay, but he wouldn't let her. He pulled away and stood up.

"I'm so sorry, Kelly; please forgive me," was the last thing he said before bolting. Kelly sat in stunned disbelief long after the door closed behind him.

✳ ✳ ✳

The next day, Kelly and Martha met for their consultation. *Thank God, we had this weekend already planned*, Kelly thought. Never had she needed it more. She hadn't slept a wink the night before. She'd tried to call Brian but he wasn't answering his phone.

After going through the whole story, Kelly sat sniffling while Martha held her hand. She blew her nose and asked "What am I going to do?"

Martha gave her a comforting hug. "Kelly, I'm so sorry. This is painful emotionally, but the first thing I want to say is: *don't make it more than it is.*"

"What do you mean?" Kelly was puzzled.

"Right now, you're tempted to elevate an emotional situation, but let's look at this rationally."

"How can I look at this rationally? My fiancé, the love of my life, called off our wedding!"

"I don't think your wedding is really off."

"But he told me he was having second thoughts, and then he bolted! He's not answering his phone or his email." Kelly spoke in a despairing voice. "The worst part is I desperately want to be there for him and I can't."

Martha touched her arm. "Hear me out, Kelly. How upset was Brian last night, on a scale of one to ten, if you had to say?"

"He was a nine or a ten. I don't think I've ever seen a guy so upset."

"Okay, now if he was that upset, how rational do you think he was at that moment?"

"He wasn't. He had his ex-wife's death mixed up with his competency as a husband. It was completely irrational but I couldn't get him to see that."

"Okay, if Brain wasn't rational last night, but he normally is, how do you think he's going to feel when his emotions calm down?"

"Terrible! He's going to feel very bad about pushing me away."

"So is Brian *really* gone, or is he temporarily freaked out by a painful situation?"

Kelly sighed. "He's freaked out. I know what it feels like when a guy really leaves, and this doesn't feel that way. In fact, if I stop and close my eyes, it's almost like I can feel him nearby. That sounds strange, doesn't it?"

"Not to me," Martha said, smiling.

Kelly's face clouded over again. "But why push me away over a situation he can't control? I could comfort him, help him deal with this, if he'd let me. Cheryl's death is awful, but he's told me over and over that I'm the love of his life. Why would he give that up?"

"I don't think he has. But more importantly, do you have room in your heart for Brian to stumble around a bit from time to time? Or does he have to be a perfect guy who never makes mistakes?"

"Of course he can make mistakes. I love him so much. I don't want him to feel like he has to be perfect for me. I certainly can't be perfect for him, and he gives me so much latitude with all of my flaws." She smiled through her tears and sniffles thinking about all of the little ways Brian made her feel completely accepted, warts and all.

"So it's fair to say Brian's afraid and that he's stumbling around right now trying to get past it. Can you see that he's afraid of not being a good husband to you, as opposed to rejecting you?"

"Yes."

"Okay, now here's the crucial question. *Do you trust Brian?* Do you trust him as a person of emotional strength and character, who can take care of his own emotional world when it gets off balance?"

Creating Real Love: Lessons In Trust

Kelly pondered Martha's question, one she'd never reflected on before, certainly not about the men in her past. None of her relationships had ever reached this point before, this deep kind of love that seemed to stretch backward before they met and forward to the end of time. She'd *wanted* to trust the men in her past; in fact, she'd foolishly trusted men who were not trustworthy, out of desperation to be loved. Brian, however, she trusted with her whole heart, without reservation, not because she needed to but because she knew she could.

"I trust him completely, there's no question about that. I want to help him get through this. Isn't that my job as his mate?"

"Your job is not to rescue, Kelly, but to be supportive. If you trust him, if you believe he's strong enough to handle his own emotional world, then the best support might be keeping your faith and love intact while he works through this.

"Most people think trust is about honesty or fidelity, but it's much more than that. It's about trusting each another to take care of your own inner world, to do the right things and make good choices. It's about consistency and keeping your word. That's why pacing is so important when you're dating. You need time and observable behavior to understand a person's ability to make good choices and keep his word. You've invested that time, Kelly, and you've learned that Brian is trustworthy. True?"

> "Trust is about much more than honesty and fidelity. It's about trusting each another to take care of your own inner worlds, to do the right things, make good choices, and keep your word."

"Yes, absolutely." Kelly didn't even hesitate.

"Then your support might be to simply trust him to come back in his own timing, to make things right in his own way. Support might be to not lose faith, put pressure on him, or try to control his emotions. How does that sound to you?"

"It sounds like the loving thing to do, but is it enough? Will he feel like I'm not there for him in his hour of need if I don't do something more, I guess, proactive?"

"Kelly, *you* might feel that way at a time like this. Women generally look for direct emotional support during crisis. But think about this. Men don't generally seek that, not the way women do. Plus, he's an independent, strong thinker. Put yourself in his shoes and tell me how he's most likely feeling."

"You're right, Martha. He'd want to work this out on his own." Kelly sighed. "I just feel so helpless. I wish there was something I could do."

"I know you do, but this is where trust really comes into play—when you feel helpless and things are out of your control. This is a test of your faith in Brian, but more importantly, it's a test of your faith in things working out the way they need to, without you trying to control the outcome.

"It's also a test of what kind of marriage you want. Do you want the role of rescuing him from his feelings, always making everything okay for him? What impact will that have on him as a man?

"Not a good one," Kelly said.

"On the other hand, do you want a marriage in which you trust him to take care of his own fears, to do the right thing, to ask for support when he needs it?"

"Yes, I do."

"What is the right thing for you to do?"

"Be patient," Kelly said, feeling decidedly the opposite.

"If you want a trusting marriage, sit tight; let him know that it's okay for him to do what he feels is right; if that is to call off the wedding, then that's what he should do.

"Be calm and level-headed," Martha said as Kelly's eyes widened. "Tell him you're disappointed but that you love him and want the best for him. Sometimes men get the emotional flu, especially divorced men right before they re-marry. Minimize the drama, be supportive, but don't rescue or push him.

"Not all paths to the altar are straight lines, Kelly. Some are crooked, with speed bumps along the way. Bottom line: *are you happy with him? Do you believe him when he says you're the one? Is his character good?* If so, then hang in there, give him space, and let him come to terms with this.

"If it turns out we're wrong about Brian and he *doesn't* come through, if he caves in to his fear, what does that tell you?"

"That we wouldn't have had a good marriage," Kelly said. "It would break my heart, but I'd rather know now than later if he doesn't have the courage to get through emotional obstacles in a relationship."

Later, after they wrapped up, Kelly drove home in a much better frame of mind. Though tired, she was serene in the knowledge that everything would work out one way or the other.

* * *

Kelly was sound asleep when the phone rang that night. It was Brian. He sounded sad but no longer distant. "I miss you," he said. "I feel terrible about leaving the way I did. I'm not sure what the right thing to do is at this point and I'm still trying to figure it out." He paused. "Are you okay?"

"I'm okay. I miss you too," Kelly said, deliberately keeping her response calm but straight from her heart. She sat up in bed so she could focus and speak rationally. "Sweetheart, I want you to know something." She paused, gathering her thoughts. "I'm really okay and I will be okay, no matter what happens. I want you to do what you feel you have to do, and even though I will grieve terribly if I lose you, that's not a good enough reason for you to marry me.

"It won't work unless you're really sure it's what you want and that you're ready to take the risk. Love isn't enough. We need to be ready for the reality that life is unpredictable and messy. We need to be confident that our bonds are strong enough to weather whatever comes our way. If one of us isn't certain about that, then we should re-think our plans."

> *"Love alone isn't enough. Life is unpredictable and messy. You need to be confident that your relationship is strong enough to weather life's storms."*

The line was silent. Brian seemed to take in what Kelly said.

"You're right. I messed up once and it was one of the worst things I've ever been through. I don't want to do that to you. I need to get my head on straight about this.

"I'll call you in a few days. Please don't give up on me. I promise you I'm doing everything I can to clear my head and you'll be the first to know when I get it straight.

"I love you, Kelly."

"I love you too, Brian. Don't worry about me. Take all the time you need."

* * *

Three days later, Kelly's doorbell rang. Her heart jumped into her throat. She looked through the peep hole in her door but all she could see was a mass of color. She opened the door and Brian handed her a huge bundle of flowers. She pulled him inside, took the flowers and set them down on a nearby table, then flung her arms around him.

"Kelly, please forgive me," Brian said, hugging and kissing her fiercely. "Please say you'll still marry me," he begged as he planted kisses all over her face and neck.

She didn't answer immediately. She sat down with him, holding his hands, and gazed intently into his eyes.

"Tell me where you are. What's happened?"

"I think I went temporarily insane there for a couple of days, but now that the fog is clear I can't believe I almost called off our wedding!"

"But you did. I hope you can understand that I need to know where we really stand in terms of our future together before I can re-commit."

"Of course. I just took you on a roller-coaster ride and hurt you. I promise I'll do everything in my power to make sure that you feel secure again."

Brian told her that he'd talked with his boss and mentor, Dale, the CEO of the company he worked for. Dale gave him a new perspective, after listening to Brian's story. He paused.

"I'm not proud of this, Kelly, but the main reason I felt so guilty is that I bailed on Cheryl because I didn't really love her. It wasn't just the drinking, although I hated it. The truth is that I fell out of love with her shortly after our wedding. We didn't really connect, not in the ways that mattered to me.

"Looking back, I wondered if my emotional disconnect pushed her into more alcohol." He frowned, as if he still wondered if that were true.

"What did Dale say?" Kelly asked.

"He basically said I need to put the past where it belongs before I screw up the best thing that's ever happened to me." He gazed into Kelly's eyes and the message was clear.

"I realize the past is in the past. It hurts to know that Cheryl didn't make it. Yes, I bailed on her, and I don't feel good about it, but I'm learning to forgive myself. I went to her funeral, Kelly, expecting her parents to blast me. It blew my mind. They *thanked* me, Kelly, for trying to love their daughter." He wiped away a tear.

Kelly listened to his story, holding his hand. When he finished, they sat together quietly, reflecting. Kelly broke the silence.

"Brian, I need to know how you're going to handle the curve balls life is bound to throw at us along the way. I don't want to repeat this after we're married."

"I know. I realize that I left the impression that I was running away from you and our commitment. I wasn't; I was running from me, but even that's no excuse. I shocked and surprised you, and I caused you pain. I deeply apologize to you for that.

"Please know that will never happen again. If I ever have an issue, I promise *you'll know it* because both of us should have the chance to resolve whatever issues arise in our relationship. It's a two-way street.

"Never have I wondered if you have doubts about me, and I intend to make sure that you never wonder about me. Your love and our relationship are the best things in my life. You can count on me to be there for you, Kelly, and for *us*."

Her heart felt a surge of love and peace. Never had she experienced real devotion from a man, not until now. *What a difference*, she thought, wiping away tears of joy.

Kelly and Brian held each other, whispering tenderly. They giggled all of a sudden as relief flooded in. It was time to get on with getting married.

Epilogue

Kelly stole away from the party for a moment, closing the door to the master bedroom. She carefully sat down so that her dress wouldn't wrinkle, closed her eyes, and did a silent prayer of gratitude.

Rising, she stood before the mirror and added a little lipstick, smiling to herself. Her gown was gorgeous, with simple lines and just the right amount of sparkle. Her hair spilled over her shoulders in soft curls. Her face glowed—she was truly beautiful, alive with love and joy. Her wedding day couldn't have been more perfect.

Downstairs, she found Brian looking for her. His face lit up as he crossed the room to take her hand. "Will you dance with me, my gorgeous wife?" he asked.

"Yes, my handsome husband!" Kelly declared. They swirled around the floor. The house was beautifully decorated, flowers and candles everywhere. It was the home of one of Kelly's parents' friends, warm and spacious enough to accommodate all of the guests for their reception.

Later, Kelly joined Martha for a quick hug and lots of knowing smiles. "I can't thank you enough. Without you, this wouldn't be happening." They agreed to talk more at a later time as Martha's husband approached, smiling.

"Kelly, it's so nice to finally meet you," John said, smiling as he took her hand. "I've heard so many wonderful things about you." Kelly felt drawn to John immediately. His warmth and innate kindness were apparent. *No wonder Martha is so happy, Kelly thought,* watching how John's eyes glowed when he looked at his wife.

Kelly shifted her attention back to her handsome and wonderful *husband.* She couldn't stop smiling as she swirled away in Brian's arms for another dance.

* * *

Two months later, Kelly and Martha met for their final coaching appointment, to reflect on their journey and celebrate Kelly's accomplishments.

Kelly thanked Martha for all of her help, bubbling over with gratitude. Martha smiled and took it in, then turned the tide. "Kelly, thank you. I'm so happy to walk with you on this leg of your life journey and assist you. It took a lot of courage to begin this journey. You had no idea what you were getting into when you bravely took a leap of faith. I admire you for hanging in there, for your tenacity, and for your adherence to your values every step of the way. I may have provided a map, but you changed your attitudes and behaviors, your life. Congratulations!"

Kelly glowed about her marital happiness. Martha reminded her again that she and Brian were still in the enchantment phase of love. Kelly vowed to remain vigilant and to seek counsel if things went off track.

* * *

"So now it's time to discuss your fee. Your payment for the program is to make a donation of your time to Shelley's Place, but only if you're truly willing. Though you were told that you would owe this, Kelly, it must come from your heart. I also ask for a financial donation. The final step is for you to choose the next recipient of the program."

Kelly was absolutely delighted to make her donations, both time and money. She truly believed in Martha's mission and admired her courage and commitment to turning personal tragedy into hope for others.

She was fascinated by Martha's research and asked more questions. In addition to her college studies, Martha had visited shelters for abused women, interviewing those who were willing. She'd looked for common threads in their stories, creating solutions through Shelley's Place, focusing on self-esteem and resource building.

Martha had also looked for and discovered a whole world full of good, loving, kindhearted men. She had talked with them, asked questions, and developed a strong faith in their existence and in the contributions they made to the world.

Kelly wanted to know every possible detail about how the group homes worked. After that, they wrapped up. Their good-bye was tearful, though they promised to stay in touch.

✳ ✳ ✳

That night, Kelly told Brian about the program, and her commitment to assist in Martha's mission. Brian expressed gratitude that Martha had helped her and insisted they celebrate her "graduation." He took her out, gave her a card and gift, and even a rolled-up diploma he made himself.

One week later, a curious email arrived in the inbox of Ashley, one of Kelly's acquaintances. The subject line read: "Sharing the Temptations with You—a Gift."

One and a half years later Kelly and Brian strolled hand in hand along the beach. The warm waves of the Caribbean splashed over their ankles. The sun slowly dipped into the ocean, blazing deep red just before it disappeared.

Brian stopped her, wrapping his arms around her and nuzzling her neck. He held her from behind, placing his hands gently over her belly. They smiled, wondering out loud if little Carl was asleep or awake. She was due in two months. Kelly closed her eyes and reflected quietly on their life together and her progress.

It wasn't perfection, not by any means! Career stress, family obligations, and pregnancy had definitely brought out their personality flaws. One by one, though, they tackled them together. They chose to emphasize their strengths as a team. After their arguments, they made it a priority to re-connect. They apologized when it was called for.

Kelly sighed, smiling to herself. It wasn't perfect but it was wonderful, absolutely wonderful, to love and be loved. Suddenly it hit her: *My vision statement*, she thought, smiling. *I'm living my vision.*

Appendix

The Temptations and the Solutions

<u>First temptation</u>: *Denial of your true desires*

The solution: Be honest with yourself: you <u>do</u> want a loving, committed relationship that leads to marriage.

<u>Second temptation</u>: *Loving a wounded guy*

The solution: Hold out for a healthy guy who's your equal in every way.

<u>Third temptation</u>: *Dating without integrity*

The solution: Make choices you can feel proud of, that are true to your deepest values.

<u>Fourth Temptation</u>: *Choosing high-risk relationships*

The solution: Make <u>you</u> your top priority: pay fierce attention to the warning bells that tell you a relationship isn't in your best interest. When it's not, move on!

<u>Fifth temptation</u>: *Settling for less*

The solution: Remain carefully detached until you meet a real candidate for marriage.

<u>Sixth temptation</u>: *Aiming for the fairy tale*

The solution: Get real! Be yourself and look for the same level of authenticity in a guy. Aim for connection at the level of core values, not skin-deep stuff that doesn't last.

Seventh Temptation: *Getting sexual too soon*

The solution: Postpone sex for at least six months while you really get to know a guy. Avoid sex unless there's real love and commitment.

Eighth temptation: *Rushing into relationships*

The solution: Pace a relationship for real discovery and take a "we'll see" attitude while it unfolds. Employ a smart dating strategy: date lots of guys for a short time without getting emotionally intense or sexual; hold out for a really great guy!

Ninth temptation: *Taking the lead*

The solution: Let the guy lead, especially in the beginning. Pay close attention to the behavior that reveals his real intentions. Decide if you want what he's offering but don't kid yourself: what you see is what you get, and what he offers up front is as good as it gets!

Tenth temptation: *Sacrificing authenticity to get the guy.*

The solution: Tell guys the truth: you're marriage-minded; be real, be honest, (never desperate!) and let the chips fall where they may. Address red flags powerfully and authentically.

How to Avoid the Temptations

- Develop and adhere fiercely to self-care and self-love.

- Get your priorities in order: spiritual inner compass and self-care first, healthy relationship second, and children only when the first two are solid.

- Create a powerful vision statement and read it every day; commit yourself to making it a reality.

- Develop a personal mantra that helps you remain detached from the outcomes of relationships and focused on the long-term vision you are aiming for.

- Be ready and willing to end any relationship at any point if you realize it's not right for you.

- Look for common values by assessing past and present behavior, not just words.

- Align your behavior to reflect your values, not your emotions.

- Be fearless: challenge and question him when necessary. How he reacts to you will be an important indicator of his character.

- With even the best of candidates, keep an open-mind; don't rush into marriage!

Date Smart

- First few dates: short timeframe, meet at the venue, avoid alcohol.

- Ask background questions, broad brushstrokes at first, delving deeper second, third, fourth dates and from there.

- Interview him for past behavior as a predictor of behavior with you; ask the key question: *How long since your last relationship and how did it end?* Listen for:

- Signs that he's still emotionally involved with the last woman (anger, resentment, longing, sadness)

- How he treated the women in his past

- Signs that he loves when he's involved

- Respect for women, even women who dumped him

- Signs that he blames women for relationship failures vs. sharing the responsibility

- Pace the relationship: infrequent, short dates for several weeks, gradually longer dates more frequently.

- Put off sex for a minimum of six months.

- Play it safe with internet dating (meeting someone online via chat room or dating service):

- Arrive early at restaurants and leave late so he can't see your license plate or follow you home.

- Meet only in public places where there are lots of people around until you feel comfortable that he is safe.

- Don't give away personal information until you really know him.

- Don't invite him to your place until you meet some of his friends, check his references, and do a background check.

About the Author

Nina Atwood is a licensed therapist and the author of three previous self-help relationship books, including the highly successful *Be Your Own Dating Service: A Step-by-Step Guide to Finding and Maintaining Healthy Relationships* (Owl Books, 1996). She is a nationally known expert resource on romantic love and singles issues, quoted in numerous publications such as the Wall Street Journal, Men's Health, Health Magazine, Glamour, Cosmopolitan, Cosmo Girl, and many more. She's been interviewed on hundreds of radio shows and as well as local and regional television shows.

Nina lives in Dallas, Texas with her husband, Mark.

Join Nina's hit website community Singlescoach® for daily tips, techniques, inspiration, guidance, personalized coaching, and much more! See www.singlescoach.com.

For additional resources, see
www.temptationsofthesinglegirl.com.

Media:
To schedule interviews with Nina, contact her directly:

Nina Atwood
5930-E Royal Lane #143
Dallas, TX 75230
214-739-2728
nina@ninaatwood.com

Special author's note:

S helley's Place is loosely modeled after Our Friends Place, a group home for girls who are at risk due to abandonment, abuse, or neglect. To find out more, go to www.ourfriendsplace.org.

LaVergne, TN USA
14 December 2009
166932LV00004B/6/A